Oscar Israelowitz's

LOWER EAST SIDE TOURBOOK

Sixth Edition

ISRAELOWITZ PUBLISHING
P.O. Box 228
Brooklyn, NY 11229
Tel. (718) 951-7072

Printed by MORIAH OFFSET CO. 718—693-3800

Contents

Introduction

The *Lower East Side Tourbook* is designed for the tourist as well as for the local resident. The international traveler will be stimulated by Orchard Street with its myriad assortment of shops and boutiques and will be reminded of the shopping bazaars in such international ports-of-call as the Souk in Jerusalem, Petticoat Lane in London's East End, or the Casbah in Tangiers. The local residents still flock down to the Lower East Side on Sundays, where several streets are actually closed to vehicular traffic and become pedestrian promenades.

All visitors to the Lower East Side have common goals. They all wish to experience the "tourist attractions." Afterall, this is where it all began—for hundreds of thousands of immigrants whose first home in America, the "Golden Land," were the teaming tenements of the Lower East Side. Visitors wish to find that special bargain or *metziya* (in Yiddish) while shopping in the Lower East Side.

You will find an assortment of very shabby turn of the century stores, sometimes located several steps below street level, filled to the brim with merchandise—literally, from wall-to-wall and floor-to-ceiling. Right next door you might find a chic boutique carrying the latest fashions from Italy or France.

The first section of this tourbook is devoted to a do-it-yourself walking tour of the Lower East Side. The numbers on the map correspond to the stop numbers on the walking tour. You may start at any point and visit the sites at your leisure.

The second section of this tourbook consists of detailed street maps dating from 1914. Each map shows all of the buildings in the neighborhood, including tenements, schools, major synagogues, etc. It is an invaluable tool for someone who wishes to find a particular address, building or perhaps do a genealogical survey. Some of the streets on these old maps no longer exist. They have been replaced with high-rise housing projects.

This section also contains a listing of over five hundred synagogues which existed in the Lower East Side in 1921. The listing is by street address followed by the name of the congregation. Some tenement buildings housed as many as six individual congregations!

Some of the old congregation names reflect the cities and villages (*shtetls*) which were left behind in the "Old Country." Most of these villages in Eastern Europe were destroyed by the Nazis during the Holocaust. The names of these communities and congregations have therefore been memorialized in this book.

There's so much to see and do in the Lower East Side, so let's begin.

How to Get There

By Car:
Take the FDR Drive (north or south) and exit at Houston Street or at Grand Street (southbound only).
Parking: Please read all parking signs carefully. All parking meter rules are active on Sundays. You *must* feed the meters on Sundays! There are several municipal parking lots and buildings along Essex Street, on either side of Delancey Street. There are several private parking lots near Allen and/or Houston Streets. There are free parking lots located on the south side of Delancey Street (directly opposite Ratner's, between Norfolk and Suffolk Streets).

By Subway:
• Take the "F" train to East Broadway, Delancey Street, or Second Avenue stations.
• Take the "B," "Q," or "D" train to Grand Street.
• Take the "J," "M," or "Z" train to Essex Street.

By Bus:
• Take the "M15" along Allen Street. This bus starts uptown and goes down Second Avenue.
• Take the "M101" or "M102" along the Bowery. This bus starts uptown and goes down Third Avenue (south of 23rd Street).

Early Jewish Settlers

In the 1650s, Holland was an international power, with colonies in the New World–in North and South America. In 1654, the Jewish community in Recife, Brazil was expelled by the new Portuguese regime which had just captured the city from the Dutch. The Jews were members of the Dutch West India Company, an international trading concern with headquarters in Amsterdam, Holland and branches in the colonies of Recife, Surinam, Curaçao, St. Eustatius, Jamaica, St. Martin and Barbados. There were small Jewish communities with individual synagogues in each of these islands and countries during the 17th and 18th centuries. Some synagogues and remains of synagogues can still be found.

The Jewish refugees of this "Portuguese Inquisition" set sail for lands offering religious freedom. Some found refuge in the Caribbean islands of Curaçao, Jamaica and Barbados. Others returned to their home port–Amsterdam, Holland. One ship heading back to Europe was attacked on the high seas of the Caribbean by Spanish pirates. The Jews were relieved of most of their valuables and dropped off on a tropical island. A French galleon, the *St. Catherine,* rescued these castaways. The ship was headed for Montreal, Quebec but dropped off its Jewish passengers in the Dutch colony of New Amsterdam (later called New York).

The *St. Catherine* docked in the harbor of New Amsterdam in September, 1654. The twenty-three Jewish refugees were greeted by the notoriously anti-Semitic governor of the colony, Peter Stuyvesant. He had no wish to harbor these penniless Jews in his colony. They were placed under arrest until orders from Stuyvesant's superiors arrived from Amsterdam. Many of the shareholders of the Dutch West India Company were Jewish and applied pressure on Governor Stuyvesant to let these refugees remain in the colony. The only provision for their release from prison was that they should not be a "burden on the community." They had to take care of their own people. Assistance did arrive for these Jews from the established communities in Amsterdam, London and Curaçao.

The first Jewish congregation in North America was organized at this time. The Spanish and Portuguese Congregation was organized in September, 1654, just before the Jewish New Year, *Rosh Hashana*. The congregation was Sephardic and was also called *Shearith Israel* or "Remnant of Israel," since these twenty-three people felt as if they were the last Jews on earth.

The British captured New Amsterdam in 1664 and named it New York. The British did not let the congregation build a synagogue until 1730. That first synagogue was located on Mill Street (today's South William Street, in the Financial District). The Spanish and Portuguese Synagogue later moved to Crosby Street, West 19th Street and then to its present location at Central Park West and 70th Street. Its landmark synagogue building contains a replica of the original 1730 Mill Street Synagogue.

For the first two centuries after their settlement in New Amsterdam, the Jewish community in America increased very slowly. By the time of the American Revolution in 1776, of a total population of three million, only some two thousand were Jews. From the Colonial period through the early 1800s, a sizable percentage of America's Jewish community assimilated in Christian society through marriage and by lapse.

Between 1820 and 1850, about 200,000 Jews arrived from the Ashkenazic countries of Germany and Bohemia. They were fleeing from political oppression and grinding poverty. It was during this period that the Reform movement developed in Europe and in the United States.

Many of these German Jews started their business careers as peddlers. They would journey out into the country, knocking on doors of isolated farmhouses and tried to sell to the farmwives a few stockings, spools of cotton thread, needles or cheap household crockery. They worked long hours and saved every penny until they could purchase a horse and wagon, or set up a small dry goods shop. This was the start of such great stores as B. Altman's, Macy's and Bloomingdale's.

The third and largest wave of Jewish immigration came between 1881 and 1924. The new arrivals were Yiddish-speaking Jews from Russia, Poland, Galicia, Roumania and Hungary. The Russian Jews fled in the wake of the bloody pogroms instigated by the Czar's government. Oppressive laws combined with constant threat of massacre drove the Jews of Eastern Europe from their homes in tremendous numbers. When this wave of immigration was stopped by U.S. law in 1924, the Jewish population in New York City was more than 1.5 million.

Most of the immigrants did not have enough money to travel in "cabin class," a luxurious accommodation on their transatlantic ocean liners. Instead, they traveled in steerage, in the cargo holds of the ships. Greater than five million Jews arrived in New York's port between 1850 and 1924. They were processed at the Castle Clinton and Ellis Island Immigration Depots. One third of these immigrants moved to New York's Lower East Side. In order to accommodate this tremendous volume of people, developers quickly built five- and six-story walk-up tenements. It was common to find eight to ten people sharing one room in these "cold water" flats. If there was an extra room in the apartment, a boarder was taken in to help pay the rent.

During the 1920s, immigration into America was reduced to a trickle. The Jews living in the teaming tenements of the Lower East Side needed "breathing space." It was at this time that the New York subways and elevated lines were extended to the Bronx, Brooklyn and Queens. New Jewish communities grew rapidly during this period in such neighborhoods as Tremont, Fordham and along the Grand Concourse in the Bronx; Borough Park, Bedford-Stuyvesant, Flatbush and Bensonhurst in Brooklyn; and Jackson Heights, Astoria, Forest Hills and Jamaica in Queens.

In the 1990s, preservation and restoration brought young urban professionals (yuppies) back to the old and former Jewish sections of town. They are "fixing-up" the century-old brownstones and abandoned apartment houses. Areas such as Manhattan's East Village, which was once part of the old Lower East Side but in recent years was known as "Alphabet City," a major center of drugs and crime, are now being "cleaned-up."

Soho used to be the site of hundreds of sweatshops and warehouses where thousands of Jewish immigrants from the Lower East Side worked twelve to sixteen hours a day in horrid conditions. The area has recently been declared an Historic District and has been transformed into a chic residential neighborhood with trendy boutiques, cafes and art galleries. The former sweatshops are now selling as million-dollar lofts.

Young Orthodox Jewish couples are now moving back into the Lower East Side. The rents in the Co-Ops are much lower than in other parts of the city such as the Upper West Side. Transportation facilities such as subways and buses are excellent. You can walk to work if you are employed in the Financial District. There are Hebrew schools or yeshivas for boys and for girls, and there is an assortment of kosher restaurants, bakeries and pizza shops. There are now about twenty-five thousand Jews living in the Lower East Side.

WALKING
TOUR

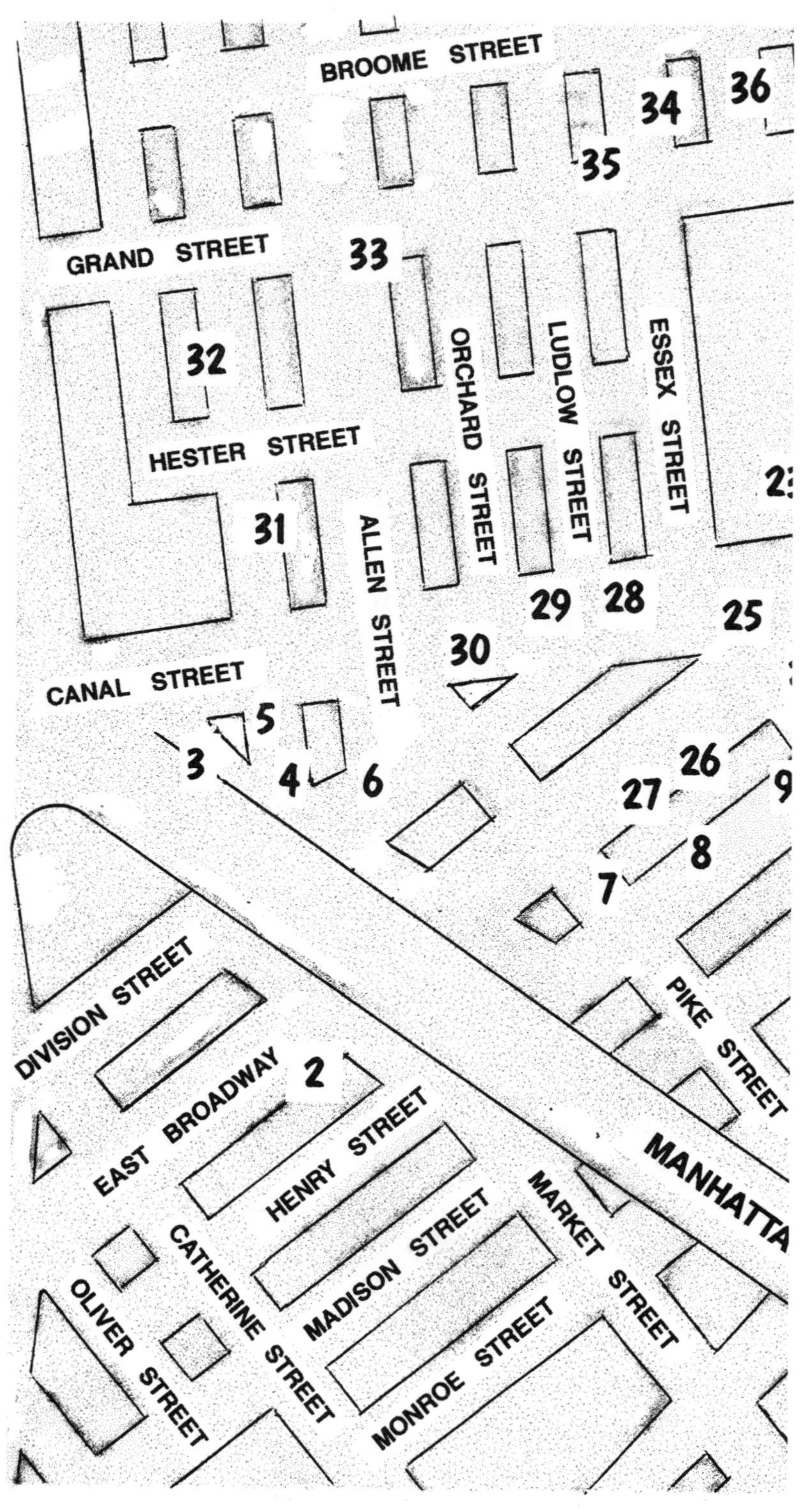

BROOME STREET
GRAND STREET
33
34
36
35
32
HESTER STREET
ORCHARD STREET
LUDLOW STREET
ESSEX STREET
23
31
ALLEN STREET
29
28
25
30
CANAL STREET
5
3
4
6
26
27
9
8
7
DIVISION STREET
EAST BROADWAY
2
HENRY STREET
MADISON STREET
MARKET STREET
MANHATTA
CATHERINE STREET
MONROE STREET
OLIVER STREET
1

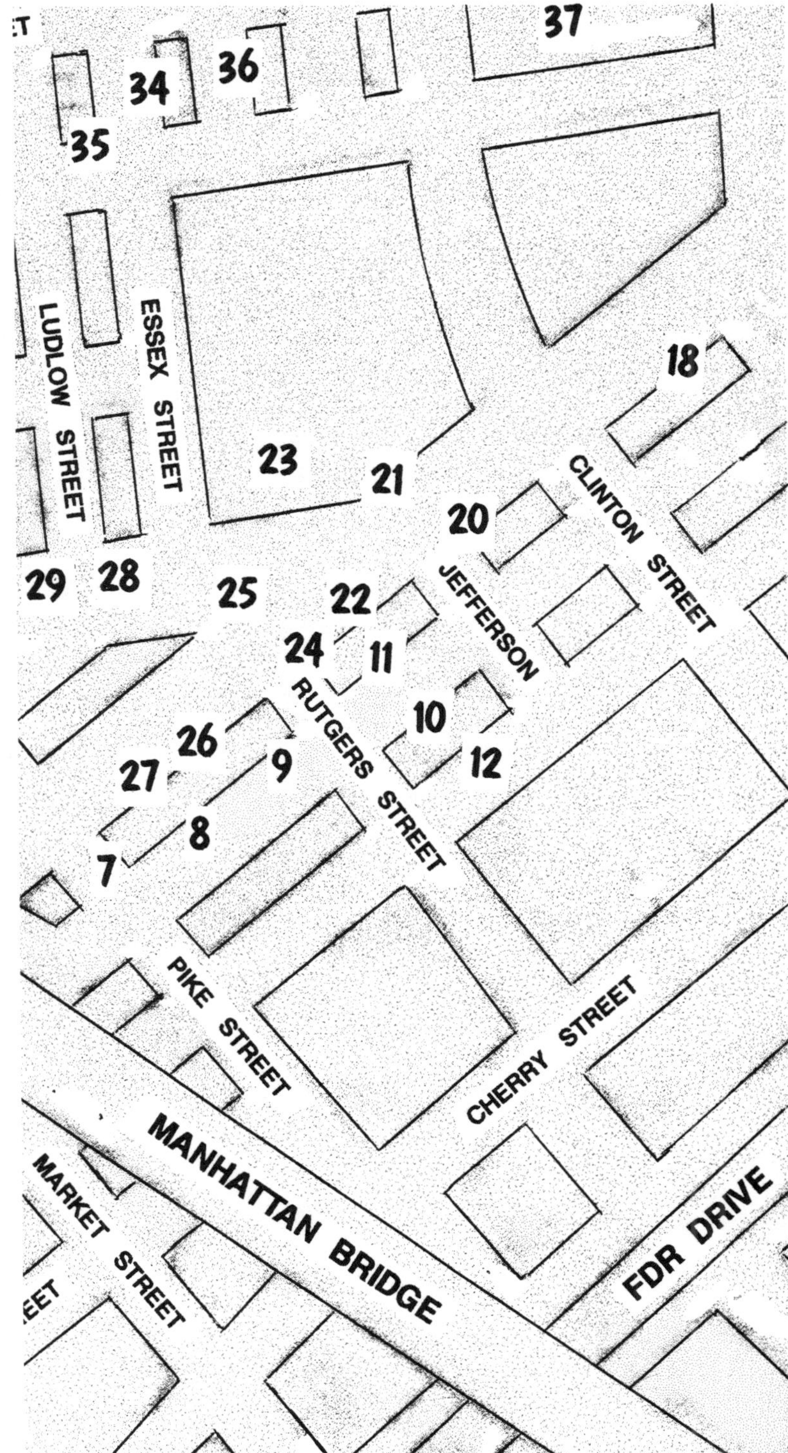
LUDLOW STREET
ESSEX STREET
CLINTON STREET
JEFFERSON
RUTGERS STREET
PIKE STREET
MARKET STREET
CHERRY STREET
MANHATTAN BRIDGE
FDR DRIVE
37
34
36
35
18
23
21
20
29
28
25
22
24
11
10
12
26
27
9
8
7

Two thirds of the 12 million immigrants arriving at Ellis Island,
moved to the Lower East Side between 1892 and 1924.

Courtesy International Museum of Photography: George Eastman House
Photo by Lewis W. Hine.

STOP 1.   **OLDEST JEWISH CEMETERY**
St. James Place near Chatham Square

The first Jewish cemetery in the United States was consecrated in 1656 in New Amsterdam. The exact location of that cemetery is unknown. The remains of the cemetery were removed to the Chatham Square burial grounds. It was acquired in 1682. Benjamin Bueno de Mesquita, who died in 1683, was the first person to be buried there.

The cemetery played an important part in the American defense of New York in 1776. It was fortified by the patriots as one of the defenses of the city. Among the graves in the cemetery are those of 18 Revolutionary soldiers and patriots. These include Hayman Levy, Isaac Moses, and Gershom Mendes Seixas, minister of Congregation Shearith Israel, who closed the only synagogue in the city and removed the Torahs to Stratford, Connecticut, when British forces occupied New York.

This is one of three Jewish cemeteries in Manhattan which belong to North America's oldest congregation, Shearith Israel, also known as the Spanish and Portuguese Synagogue. The other two cemeteries are located on West 11th Street (just east of Sixth Avenue) and on West 21st Street (just west of Sixth Avenue).

STOP 2.   **SITE OF RABBI ISAAC ELCHANAN THEOLOGICAL SEMINARY**
47 East Broadway

Named after Rabbi Isaac Elchanan Spektor,

a prominent scholar from Kovno, Lithuania, the Theological Seminary was the forerunner of today's Yeshiva University. It was organized in 1886 at 47 East Broadway, then moved to East Broadway and Montgomery Street, and is today located at its main campus in the Washington Heights section of Manhattan.

STOP 3. **SAINT BARBARA GREEK ORTHODOX CHURCH**
27 Forsyth Street

This building was originally designed as a synagogue, Congregation Mishkan Israel Suwalki, in 1895.

The first distinct Jewish neighborhood arose in the 1870s at the corner of Bayard and Mott Streets (now in the heart of Chinatown). These people were skilled tailors from Suwalki and Great Poland (located near the German border). There is a red brick tenement structure at Bayard and Elizabeth Streets which displays Stars of David on its façade.

These Jews later moved to the area near Canal and Essex Streets. They organized a congregation during that period and built the magnificent synagogue at 27 Forsyth Street, just opposite today's Manhattan Bridge entrance. That building is still extant but is now used by Saint Barbara Greek Orthodox Church.

STOP 4. **ELDRIDGE STREET SYNAGOGUE RESTORATION PROJECT**
14 Eldridge Street   Tel. (212) 219-0888

The Eldridge Street Shul is a National Historic Landmark.

Courtesy of the Rabbi William A. Rosenthall Collection

Built by Eastern European immigrants in 1886, the Eldridge Street Synagogue, Congregation Kahal Adas Jeshurun Anshei Lubz, was created by a merger of two congregations, Adas Jeshurun and Anshei Lubz. It was the first major Orthodox synagogue built specifically as a synagogue in the Lower East Side. Other congregations such as the Bialystoker Shul, the Roumaniashe Shul and the Beth Hamedrash Hagadol simply purchased former churches and converted them into synagogues.

Some of the founding fathers of the Eldridge Street Shul included Isaac Gellis (of hot-dog fame) and Sandor Jarmulowsky, noted for his high-rise bank building located at the corner of Orchard and Canal Streets. Yossele Rosenblatt was once the cantor of this synagogue. A young Eddie Cantor once sang in the choir of the Eldridge Street Shul. His home was located just across the street, at 19 Eldridge Street.

The synagogue was designed by the Herter Brothers. They also designed several tenement buildings in the late 1880s using their unique signature, Stars of David engraved on the façades. The architectural style of the Eldridge Street Shul is a mixture of Gothic, Romanesque and Moorish.

The main sanctuary is an immense and opulent hall with elaborate brass chandeliers with Victorian glass shades hanging in the middle of a huge barrel-vaulted space. The space is as glorious as the Great Synagogue in Florence, Italy. The Ark was designed in Italian walnut. The details on the Ark closely resemble those found on the Ark of Pittsburgh's Beth Hamedrash Haga-

The Eldridge Street Synagogue was built in 1886.

dol Beth Jacob Congregation, which was built in 1873.

When the $8 million restoration project is completed, the Eldridge Street Synagogue will function as a synagogue/museum. There will be daily prayer services in the morning and evening. Other times, during "business hours," the synagogue will function as a Jewish museum with educational programs and tours, open to the general public.

There have been continuous weekly religious services in this synagogue since it was built in 1886. Even during major structural renovations, with steel beams reinforcing the ceiling of the *bais hamedrash* (daily chapel), there *were* Sabbath services. All participants in the minyan, however, were required to wear "hard hats" during the prayer services!

The Eldridge Street Synagogue was declared a National Historic Landmark in 1996.

STOP 5.   **HOME OF EDDIE CANTOR**
19 Eldridge Street

Located directly across the street from the Eldridge Street Synagogue, is the tenement home of the radio and movie personality. Eddie Cantor. He took acting and voice lessons at the Educational Alliance (197 East Broadway) to improve his acting and singing career. His photograph is hanging in the lobby of that institution, on a wall called "Hall of Famers," along with other great personalities who took classes at the Educational Alliance. Just for fun, try to find a Star of David as part of a mosaic floor design in a nearby tenement entrance.

STOP 6.   **MANHATTAN RAILWAY COMPANY
ELECTRICAL SUBSTATION**
100 Division Street (NW corner Allen St.)

This facility served the Second Avenue El (elevated train) which ran from the Brooklyn Bridge, along Allen Street, turned at 23rd Street, and continued up along Second Avenue. It had a spur at the 59th Street Queensboro Bridge. Part of that spur is visible at either end of the bridge. The Second Avenue El continued to the Bronx.

Allen Street was originally as narrow as Orchard and Ludlow Streets but was widened in 1930 by removing one section of tenements which faced Allen Street. When standing on Allen Street today, you can see only the "backs" of tenements which face Orchard Street.

Allen Street's perpetual darkness and noise from the Second Avenue El made it an undesirable place. It was once the city's most notorious "Red Light" district!

STOP 7.   **PIKE STREET SHUL** (former)
15 Pike Street

Congregation Sons of Israel Kalvarier was built in 1903. It was once one of the great synagogues in the Lower East Side. The first ordination ceremony of the Rabbi Isaac Elchanan Theological Seminary was held in this synagogue in 1906. Ordination (*s'micha*) was granted to three rabbis. In 1917, this congregation had an uptown branch in Harlem. Harlem was a major Jewish area, with over 178,000 Jewish inhabitants during its peak period, in the

The former Pike Street Shul has been converted into luxury apartments.

1910s.

More recently, the Pike Street Shul was the site of the funeral of Rav Aaron Kotler, prominent Torah scholar and *rosh yeshiva* (dean) of the Bais Hamedrash Gevohah in Lakewood. The funeral was attended by fifty thousand people.

In the 1970s, the congregation had dwindled down to a handful of elderly members. Some moved to Florida. There was basically no one left to run the shul. So, several of the New York members decided to sell the shul to a local Chinese church, without the knowledge or permission of the other members of the congregation who had settled in Florida. The case was brought to litigation. After several years in the courts the judge ruled that the sale was null and void.

However, during those years of litigation, the building was totally neglected. Vandals broke in on a daily basis and took out any items which were of any value, e.g. brass fixtures, plumbing fixtures, etc. The building was basically abandoned. Drug addicts moved in and conducted their business.

At this point, the city took over the building, bricked-up the front doorways and sealed-up what was left of the elegant stained-glass windows. The building went up for auction. It was purchased by a local Chinese church.

Pike Street is now part of Chinatown and the old Pike Street Shul is now a Chinese church, with a hardware store on street level.

STOP 8.   **CHEVRE MISHKAN ANSHE ZETEL**
135 Henry Street

This is one of the few remaining *shteeblech* (mini-synagogues) in the Lower East Side.

STOP 9.   **SAINT TERESA'S**
ROMAN CATHOLIC CHURCH
16-18 Rutgers Street   Tel. (212) 233-0233

This building was erected as the First Presbyterian Church of New York in 1841, when the neighborhood was still a semi-rural suburb. In 1863, when the neighborhood was becoming heavily Irish, the building was purchased by the Archdiocese, and it has been a Roman Catholic church ever since. It now serves the Hispanic and Oriental groups of the neighborhood. Masses are conducted in Spanish, Chinese and English.

STOP 10.   **FORMER SYNAGOGUE**
156 Henry Street

This building was built for Congregation Agudas Anshe Mamud u'Bais Va'ad Lachachamim in 1904. The congregation moved to the Home of the Sages at 283 East Broadway. It sold its original building to a Chinese church. The Stars of David are still visible in the large circular windows.

STOP 11.   **SITE OF YESHIVA**
RABBI JACOB JOSEPH
203 Henry Street

In 1899, Rabbi Jacob Joseph from Vilna, Lithuania, was appointed "Chief Rabbi" of the City of New York. This designation was met with much resistance and lasted only several months. He was also rabbi of the

Beth Hamedrash Hagadol, located at 60 Norfolk Street.

The yeshiva or Hebrew school, named in his honor, was built in 1913 and was known as RJJ. It was one of the most prominent learning institutions in the city. In 1976, the yeshiva moved to Staten Island. The two buildings stood empty for several years. They were ultimately purchased by a developer who renovated them into residential apartments. The original Hebrew and English name entablatures of the yeshiva were left intact on the front façade.

The small playground just to the left of the former RJJ Yeshiva, on the corner of Rutgers Street, was named in memory of Captain Jacob Joseph, the grandson of the Chief Rabbi, who was killed-in-action as a United States Marine in Guadacanal during World War II.

STOP 12. **FORMER SYNAGOGUE**
209 Madison Street

This tenement-style synagogue belonged to Congregation Etz Chaim Anshe Volozin. It closed in 1989 and was renovated into residential apartments.

STOP 13. **HENRY STREET SETTLEMENT**
263-267 Henry Street   Tel. (212) 766-9200

The Henry Street Settlement was founded in 1893 by Lilian Wald, the pioneer social worker. The agency was originally called the Nurses' Settlement. Lilian Wald was a nurse as well and organized what is still known today as the Visiting Nurse Service, which has assisted thousands of sick people in their homes.

The elegant Greek Revival town houses, built in 1832, were donated to the Henry Street Settlement by Jacob H. Schiff, one of the wealthiest and most prominent of the "Uptown" Jewish philanthropists associated with the Educational Alliance.

Note the exquisite town houses with dormers just around the corner, on Grand and Clinton Streets. They were built in the 1820s and 1830s.

STOP 14.   **SAINT AUGUSTINE'S CHAPEL**
290 Henry Street   Tel. (212) 673-5300

Originally known as All Saints Church, it was built between 1827 and 1829 in the Federal style. Its fieldstone design is similar to the Willett Street Methodist Church, which was built in 1826 but is now used by the Bialystoker Synagogue.

This church was designed with an upstairs slave gallery into which black slaves were shackled while their white owners worshiped below. The original iron shackles were recently removed from the upper galleries.

The story is told of "Boss" William Marcy Tweed, who headed the infamous ring which drained New York City's treasury in the 1860s and 1870s. At the time of his mother's death, Tweed was a fugitive from justice, but nevertheless he attended her funeral in this church by hiding himself in the old slave gallery.

STOP 15.   **EAST SIDE TORAH CENTER**
313 Henry Street

This institution celebrated its 100th anniversary in 1990. There are several historic plaques along the building's façade commemorating this event.

STOP 16.   **EAST SIDE MIKVEH - RITUALARIUM**
313 East Broadway   Tel. (212) 475-8514

Built in 1904 as the Arnold Toynbee Hall, this structure served as a settlement house which provided educational and recreational activities for the newly-arrived immigrants in the Lower East Side. The initials of the original institution "ATH" still appear in the stone balustrade over what had once been the main entrance.

The building later housed the Young Men's Benevolent Association. Recently, the building was purchased and restored by the nearby Gouverneur Hospital. It houses administrative offices.

The mikveh is still functioning as well. A mikveh or ritual bath is an important part of life for Orthodox Jewish women, who must attend as part of the preparation for marriage, and who are required to cleanse themselves in it every month.

STOP 17.   **AMALGAMATED DWELLINGS**
Grand, Broome, Willett and Lewis Streets

The Amalgamated Dwellings are also known as the Sidney Hillman Houses. They were an early experiment in cooperative housing, built in 1930 under the auspices of the Amalgamated Clothing Workers of

America. It has a central garden with a fountain. The scale is modest and humane, and the overall effect is altogether civilized and dignified. It was designed by the architectural firm of Springsteen and Goldhammer.

STOP 18. **SHTEEBLE ROW**
225-283 East Broadway

Between 1880 and 1924 more than two million Jews emigrated to New York City. They arrived with their entire families and, in some instances, with their entire communities. They established brotherly aid societies (*landsmanschaften*), burial societies and synagogues.

In its peak, around the turn of the century, the Lower East Side had over 600,000 Jewish immigrants and over five hundred synagogues. Many of these synagogues were not free-standing structures. Rather, they were apartments in tenements or renovated store-fronts converted into mini-synagogues. The term for such a small synagogue is *shteeble*, a Yiddish word meaning "small room."

The second section of this tourbook contains the master list of many of these small synagogues. Sometimes, as many as five or six separate congregations were housed in one tenement building. Some synagogues were named after the cities or villages (*shtetls*) in Eastern Europe. Other congregations were organized by various trades e.g. shoemakers, plumbers, tailors, etc., and were known by such names as the *"Tailor's Shul."*

The question remains, "Why were there so

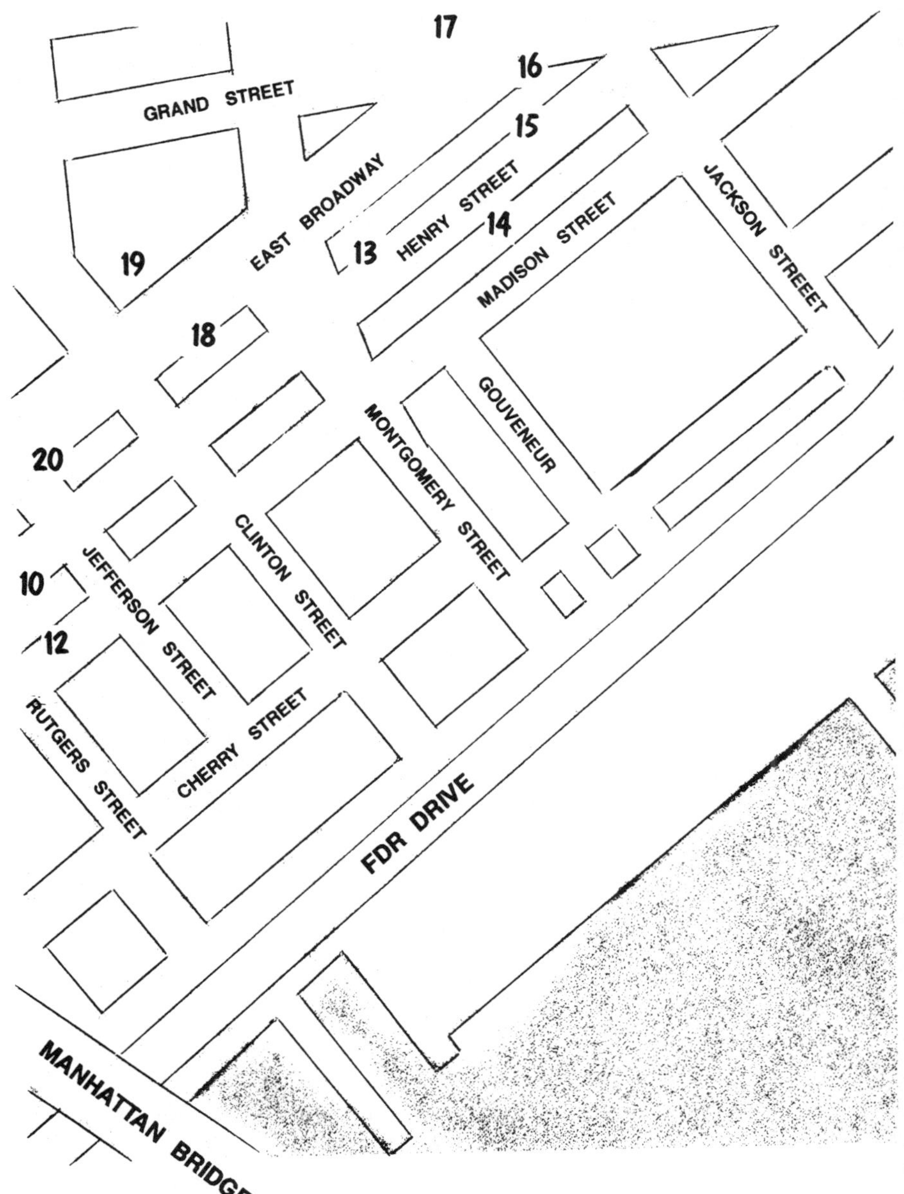

17
16
15
14
13
GRAND STREET
EAST BROADWAY
HENRY STREET
MADISON STREET
JACKSON STREEET
GOUVENEUR
MONTGOMERY STREET
CLINTON STREET
JEFFERSON STREET
CHERRY STREET
RUTGERS STREET
FDR DRIVE
MANHATTAN BRIDGE
19
18
20
10
12

many congregations?" The answer may lie in the classic tale of a shipwrecked castaway. After several years on a desert island, a ship came along and rescued this lone Jewish survivor and found an entire village, complete with shops, homes and two large synagogues. The captain asked the survivor, "Why were there two synagogues on this desert island?" He replied as he pointed to each synagogue, "This is the synagogue that I pray in every single day. And that is the synagogue that I'll never set foot into!" That may be why there were over five hundred individual congregations in the Lower East Side around the turn of the century.

There are still about a dozen shteeblech along East Broadway, between Clinton and Montgomery Streets. One of these mini-synagogues was originally located on Cannon Street. It was relocated to East Broadway in the 1950s, when Cannon Street disappeared during an Urban Renewal Project—the construction of the Co-Ops. The sign in front of this shteebl therefore provides the name of the congregation (in Hebrew) with the key phrase, *"Formerly 52 Cannon Street."*

STOP 19. **BIALYSTOKER HOME FOR THE AGED**
228 East Broadway

Designed in the 1920s in the Art Deco style, the Bialystoker Home for the Aged houses many senior citizens who arrived in the Lower East Side in the early part of this century. The twelve entablatures around the front entrance are symbolic of the twelve tribes of Israel.

JEWISH MURAL

On right side wall of the Bialystoker Home for the Aged is a mural drawn in the 1970s by the Jewish students of the Educational Alliance. The mural depicts the history of the Jewish people vis-a-vis the Lower East Side.

The upper left section of the mural depicts the immigrants arriving in New York on the ocean steamers in the late 1880s. Below that is a sign for the Jewish Daily Forward (*Forverts*, in Yiddish) which is still in publication. Below the sign is a rendering of labor union workers marching for better working conditions. Many of those rallies were held in Union Square, near 14th Street. Union Square is actually named for the Union Armies which assembled at that location and served as a staging point during the Civil War. A sister Union Square can be found in downtown San Francisco, which also served as a military staging point.

The mural depicts the logo of the International Ladies Garment Workers Union (ILGWU). That labor union, which was organized in the Lower East Side, is still functioning and was recently popularized by a catchy tune, "Look for the Union Label..."

The upper right section of the mural depicts victims of the Holocaust. The Star of David wrapped with chains is symbolic of the plight of the Soviet Jews. Since this mural was drawn in the 1970s, several hundred thousand Russian Jews have been allowed to leave Russia.

In the center of the mural is the focal point of the Jewish people—the State of Israel.

The Educational Alliance was founded in 1889.

STOP 20. **EDUCATIONAL ALLIANCE**
197 East Broadway   Tel. (212) 475-6200

Organized in 1889, the Educational Alliance was the first settlement house in the United States created by the Jewish community. It was organized by the wealthy "Uptown Jews" –members of the German-Jewish community that had itself made the Lower East Side its original home in the 1830s-1870s. These "Uptown Jews" felt an obligation to help out the newly-arrived Eastern European Jews who lived down-town, and wanted at the same time, to prevent anti-Semitism against their coreligion-ists. Some say that these "Uptown Jews" were also ashamed and embarrassed of these people who were dressed in the "Old World" garb and only spoke Yiddish.

The established German-Jewish communi-ty organized the Educational Alliance in order to quickly "Americanize" the new immigrants. There were classes in English, art, music, civics, theater, etc.

There were once huge bronze plaques in the lobby of the Educational Alliance honor-ing some of its founders. Some of these notable philanthropists included Louis Marshall, Jacob H. Schiff, Felix M. Warburg, Benjamin (B.) Altman and Isidor Straus. Straus was president of the board of trustees of the Educational Alliance from its founding in 1889 until 1912, when he and his wife went down with the *Titanic*. Isidor Straus was also the owner of Macy's Department Store.

The lobby contains its "Hall of Famers" –photographic portraits of distinguished alumni of the Educational Alliance including David Sarnoff, the young immigrant who learned English in its classes and later founded RCA; Arthur Murray, who practiced his first dance steps at Saturday night socials; Eddie Cantor, who acted and sang in theater productions; Jo Davidson and Jacob Epstein, who each paid three cents a week for lessons in sculpture and used as volunteer models the pushcart peddlers from nearby Orchard and Rivington Streets; and Chaim Gross, who took art classes here and later instructed art students of the Educational Alliance until his recent death at the age of 100. Some of Chaim Gross' lithographs are on display in the lobby.

Sholom Aleichem wrote many of his stories at a desk in the Alliance and, in 1906, appeared with Mark Twain in a joint lecture at the building's Isidor Straus Theater. The great Yiddish writer was introduced to the audience as the "Jewish Mark Twain"–to which Twain responded, "I am the American Sholom Aleichem."

The Educational Alliance is today run by the UJA-Federation and is basically a community center catering to the three dominant ethnic groups in the neighborhood; Jewish, Oriental and Hispanic. The locals call the Educational Alliance, the *"Edjees."*

STOP 21. **NEW YORK PUBLIC LIBRARY –SEWARD PARK BRANCH**
192 East Broadway

This branch of the New York Public Library was built in 1909. At that time, the area was teaming with immigrants. Tenements were built right up against each side of the library. You can still see the "ghost" of the adjoining building on the right wall. The architects decided to give the immigrants a special area where they could read their books outdoors in the fresh air. A rooftop garden with exquisite copper railings and ornaments was constructed. That rooftop garden is now closed and is just an architectural detail.

This branch of the New York Public Library still has a large selection of books in Yiddish but also has books in Chinese and Spanish, catering to all of the ethnic groups in the neighborhood.

STOP 22. **JEWISH DAILY FORWARD BUILDING**
175 East Broadway

This section of East Broadway was once known as the "Publishers Row" of the Yiddish newspaper. Five Yiddish papers were once published on this street. The largest on the block, the Jewish Daily Forward (*Forverts* in Yiddish), was founded in 1897. Its publisher from 1903 to 1951 was Abraham Cahan. He introduced a special feature called "*A Bintel Brief*" or bundle of letters, the Yiddish equivalent to a "Dear Abby" column.

The Jewish Daily Forward building, one of the largest structures in the Lower East Side, also housed the headquarters of the Workmen's Circle (*Arbiter Ring* in Yiddish), as well as many other Jewish social and benevolent organizations and burial societies (*landsmanschaften*). The building was recently sold to a Chinese church. It has been designated an official New York City landmark. That means primarily that no part of the building's exterior façades may

The Jewish Daily Forward Building housed one of the first Yiddish newspapers.

be altered. Therefore, the Yiddish name entablature at the top of the building, just below the clock, nor the Chinese lettering on the right side of the building which says, "*Jesus Saves,*" can never be removed.

The Jewish Daily Forward is still published, not as a daily paper but rather as a weekly edition. There are Yiddish and English editions of the paper. The paper and the Workmen's Circle are today located at 45 East 33rd Street, near Park Avenue.

Just a block to the left (east) of the old Jewish Daily Forward building on East Broadway is New York's other major Yiddish newspaper, the *Algemeiner Journal.* It recently returned to its roots in the Lower East Side.

STOP 23. **SEWARD PARK**
East Broadway, Canal and Essex Streets

This vest-pocket park was created in 1900 by the demolition of two blocks of tenements. This park was the place where thousands of newly-arrived immigrants would gather each dawn. Owners of nearby sweatshops would come and randomly select workers for daily employment. This daily "shape-up" was known as the "*Chazir Mark,*" a Yiddish term referring to a pig market.

A mural of this artisan's market once appeared on the wall of the old Garden Cafeteria (now the Wing Shing restaurant-located at East Broadway and Rutgers Street). That mural was to be moved to the Jewish Museum but somehow "disappeared" during the transition of ownership of the restaurant from Jewish to Chinese.

STOP 24.   **GARDEN CAFETERIA** (former)
165 East Broadway

This was the site of the landmark Jewish eatery, the Garden Cafeteria, until its sale to a Chinese restaurant in 1987. It was the meeting place for Yiddish writers, poets and actors from the 1920s through the 1960s.

STOP 25.   **NATHAN STRAUS SQUARE**
East Broadway,
southeast corner Essex Street

This square is named in honor of Nathan Straus, the philanthropist who made it possible for the poor and young to have pasteurized milk, thereby saving thousands of lives. In 1920, there were 300 Nathan Straus milk stations throughout the United States.

STOP 26.   **MESIFTA TIFERETH JERUSALEM**
145 East Broadway   Tel. (212) 964-2830

One of the last surviving yeshivas or Hebrew schools in the Lower East Side, Mesifta Tifereth Jerusalem (MTJ) was organized by the Orthodox community around the turn of the century. It is an all boys school with classes from the kindergarten level through rabbinical seminary. Originally, the student body numbered close to one thousand. Now, there are only about 250 students in all classes. The main study hall or *bais hamedrash* also functions as a synagogue, with daily services.

The last *rosh yeshiva* or dean of Mesifta Tifereth Jerusalem was the world-famous

Seward Park was created after several blocks of tenements were cleared.

Courtesy of the Museum of the City of New York

Torah scholar, Rabbi Moshe Feinstein. He passed away just before theholiday of Purim, on March 24, 1986. The funeral was held in the *bais hamedrash,* with an overflow crowd of thousands in the street outside. He was buried in Jerusalem.

There are several former yeshiva buildings in the area. The former Rabbi Jacob Joseph Yeshiva (RJJ) is located at 203 Henry Street. It moved to Staten Island in 1976. The former yeshiva buildings were renovated into residential apartments.

The old East Side Hebrew Institute, located at the corner of Avenue B and East 8th Street (opposite Tompkins Square Park), has also been converted into an apartment house.

Mesifta Tifereth Jerusalem has a branch on Staten Island. They purchased a former Catholic orphanage near the Outerbridge Crossing, at 1870 Drimgoold Road East, in the Princes Bay section.

The last yeshiva for girls in the Lower East Side, Beth Jacob, is located at 142 Broome Street.

STOP 27. **JEWISH TENEMENTS**
137-139 East Broadway

The Herter Brothers, a noted architectural firm, designed mansions along Fifth Avenue and the glorious Eldridge Street Synagogue in the Lower East Side. They were commissioned to design several tenement buildings specifically for the mass influx of Jewish immigrants in the late 1880s. The architects designed standard five-story walk-ups but initialed their buildings with terra cotta Stars of David motifs above the windows.

RABBI A. M. EISENBACH

מירושלים

סופר ומוכר ספרי תורות, תפילין ומזוזות

ומתקן תפילין מעור אחד

Importer, Dealer and Repairing of
SEFER TORAHS, TEFILIN & RELIGIOUS ARTICLES

41 ESSEX STREET • NEW YORK, N.Y. 10002

TEL.
(212) 674-8840

TEL. FAX
(212) 982-4217

These designs were never intended to signify that these buildings served a religious function but were rather just architectural ornamentations.

Other buildings designed by the Herter Brothers with similar Star of David motifs can be found at 47 Orchard Street and on Broome Street, between Mott and Mulberry Streets–in the heart of today's Little Italy! The last location has a splendid cornice designed with a sculpture of Moses.

STOP 28. **CANAL STREET THEATER** (former)
31 Canal Street

The beautifully detailed terra cotta façade of the old Canal Street Theater can be seen at 31 Canal Street. It was once a silent movie palace, built in the 1920s. The auditorium of the theater, with its side exits and fire escapes, is still visible along the Ludlow Street façade.

The main lobby of the old movie palace now houses an electric appliance store (ABC Trading Co.). The original terra cotta ornaments in the lobby of the former movie palace are still visible along the high ceiling and the side walls. The main auditorium now houses a warehouse.

STOP 29. **KLETZKER BROTHERLY AID ASSOCIATION** (former)
5 Ludlow Street

Located across the street from the former Canal Street Theater is the former Kletzker Brotherly Aid Association. It was organized by a group of Jews who came from the city of

Kletzk over one hundred years ago. This organization was known as a *landsman-schaft*–an association of people from the old town who could provide the lonely immigrant who might have just arrived without his family with moral support and funds for the basic necessities such as medical care or possibly for burial needs. Some brotherly aid societies assisted struggling businessmen or helped congregations build their own synagogues.

The building is no longer owned by the Kletzker Brotherly Aid Association, although the name entablature is still highlighted with a Star of David. The building is now utilized by a Chinese funeral parlor.

STOP 30. **JARMULOWSKY'S BANK BUILDING**
Canal and Orchard Streets

Mr. Sandor Jarmulowsky arrived in the Lower East Side in 1870. He started out selling rags from a pushcart on Hester Street. He became financially successful and founded a bank for his fellow immigrants in 1873. His bank building was erected in 1895 and was the tallest structure in the neighborhood. The bank's finances stood on shaky grounds. After the Panic of 1907 and the founder's death, the bank finally collapsed. Thousands of immigrant depositors were ruined with the bank's failure. There was no insurance on their deposits.

The building now houses a number of garment factories. Jarmulowsky's name is boldly engraved on the corner façade.

Shopping at Ridley's on Grand Street, circa 1890.

Bring Your Space to LIFE!

Sheila's Decorating Inc.

⇒ Retail & Wholesale Decorating Center ⇐

More than just Wallpaper, We're your one-stop shop for:

- Furniture
- Fabrics & Carpeting
- Decorating Service
- Wallpaper
- Window Treatments
- Installation

– Specialists in Commercial Interiors –

From wall-to-wall & floor-to-ceiling, we have what you need to beautify any space, before the showrooms and at much better prices.
Come in Sunday to Friday, 9 AM - 5 PM • Visa, MC accepted.

68 ORCHARD ST. • 212-777-3767
(CORNER OF GRAND & ORCHARD)

STOP 31. HOME OF IRA GERSHWIN
60 Eldridge Street

Ira Gershwin, brother of George Gershwin, was born at this site on December 6, 1896. Ira wrote the lyrics for nearly all of George Gershwin's songs.

STOP 32. FORMER SYNAGOGUE
87 Eldridge Street

This modified tenement building housed two separate congregations in the 1920s; Congregation Tifereth Jeshurun and Congregation Chevrah Anshei Grodno v'Anshei Staputkin.

STOP 33. RIDLEY'S DEPARTMENT STORE SITE
Southeast corner Grand & Allen Streets

Ridley's Department Store started as a small shop on this site in 1849. By the 1880s, it had expanded to become the country's largest retail store. The building covered an entire city block, from Orchard to Allen Street (before Allen Street was widened in 1930). Only one third of the original structure is still extant. Ridley's closed in 1901. Another large clothing store, located nearby at Grand Street and Broadway, was the original Lord and Taylor.

STOP 34. BIRTHPLACE OF B'NAI B'RITH
Essex Street, between Grand & Broome

About one hundred and fifty feet from the northeast corner of Grand Street is an historic plaque marking the site of the birth-place of the Jewish organization, *B'nai B'rith,* on October 13, 1843. They met in Sinsheimer's Cafe, which was once located at 60 Essex Street.

STOP 35. **SEWARD PARK HIGH SCHOOL**
350 Grand Street

Built in 1929 on the site of the old Ludlow Street Prison, Seward Park High School was named in honor of the Secretary of State, William Seward, who was responsible for the purchase of Alaska from Russia. That purchase was known as "Seward's Folly."

Among the sons of the Lower East Side who graduated from this school are actors Zero Mostel and Walter Matthau.

STOP 36. **BETH HAMEDRASH HAGADOL**
60 Norfolk Street   Tel. (212) 674-3330

Built in 1852 as the Norfolk Street Baptist Church, the Gothic Revival building was purchased in 1885 by the Orthodox Jewish congregation that is still housed in it. It is, therefore, the home of the oldest Orthodox congregation in the city continuously housed in a single location.

In 1899, Rabbi Jacob Joseph from Vilna was appointed rabbi of the congregation. He was later given the short-lived title of "Chief Rabbi" of the City of New York.

STOP 37. **CHURCH OF SAINT MARY**
440 Grand Street   Tel. (212) 674-3266

The Church of Saint Mary is the oldest Roman Catholic church structure in New

York City. It was built in 1832. The brick façade, with its wooden trims and door frames, and the twin spires, are additions dating from 1871, and were designed by the prolific church architect Patrick Charles Keely. The main part of the structure is composed of rough-hewn fieldstone (Manhattan schist), revealing the architectural (Federal) style of the 1830s.

STOP 38. **HENRY STREET SETTLEMENT PLAYHOUSE**
466 Grand Street   Tel. (212) 598-0400

This is a branch of the Henry Street Settlement. It started as a theater for the Settlement's amateur productions but soon became a house for professional theater as well. Graduates of the acting course given here include Gregory Peck, Tammy Grimes, Diane Keaton, Eli Wallach and Lorne Greene.

STOP 39. **BIALYSTOKER SYNAGOGUE**
7 Bialystoker (Willett) Street
Tel. (212) 475-0165

Built in 1826 as the Willett Street Methodist Church, the fieldstone structure is an official New York City landmark. Before the Civil War, the building was used as part of the "Underground Railroad" which smuggled black slaves from the South to "safe houses" in the North. There is a secret "trap door" located at the northwest corner on the balcony level. It has been painted over but can be seen if you look carefully.

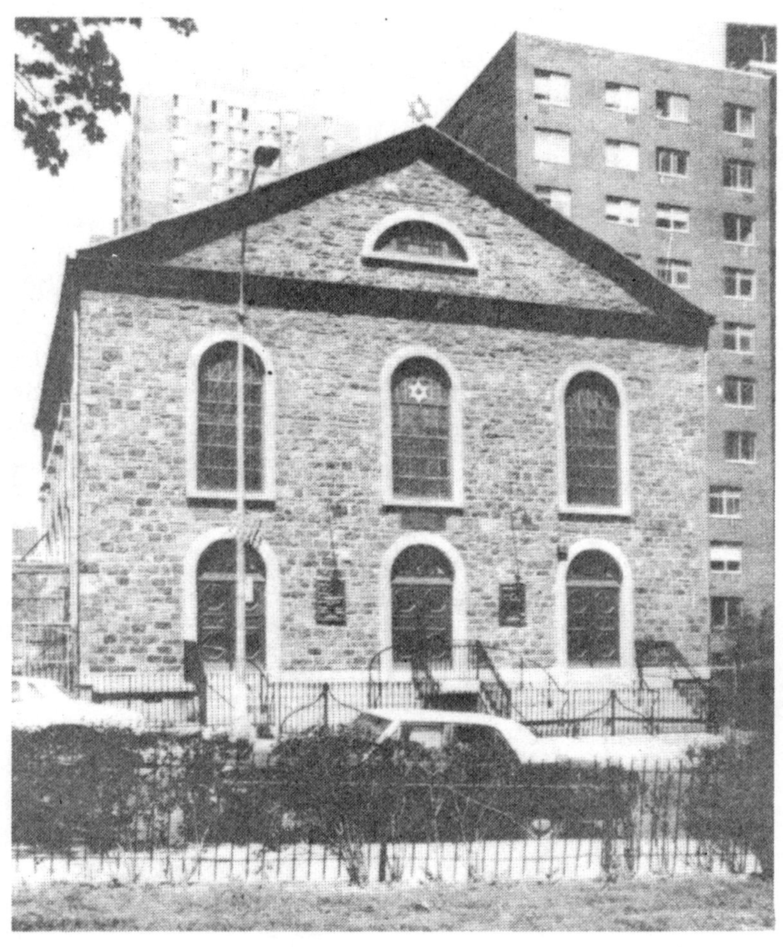

The landmark Bialystoker Synagogue.

The Orthodox Congregation Anshei Bialystok, which had been organized on Orchard Street in 1878, purchased this building in 1905. It is the oldest structure in the city to house a synagogue. The lavish Ark with its exquisite gold-leaf details was designed in Italy. There are three sculptural crowns above the Ark as well as two bold lions perched on top.

Since the building has been declared an official city landmark, the exterior façades cannot be altered. This posed a problem when the congregation wanted to install a central air conditioning unit. It was not permitted to be installed on any exterior part of the building. Two large units were therefore built *inside* the synagogue's upper balcony (east wall) and enclosed with sheetrock partitions.

The Bialystoker Synagogue was recently restored at a cost of over $250,000. The original ceiling and wall murals depicting the signs of the zodiac and scenes of Jerusalem were completely restored to their 1905 elegance.

The unique wash basin in the lobby of the synagogue was originally two oak wine barrels. They were donated by Schapiro's Winery, located on Rivington Street.

Bialystok was a major Jewish city in Poland/Russia (the borders changed hands after each war) before World War II. Be sure to see the Bialystoker Home for the Aged, located at 228 East Broadway. It is designed in the Art Deco style and has a Jewish mural on its east façade. And, of course, don't forget to buy a "Bialy" (an onion roll originating in Bialystok) at their bakery on Grand Street, near Essex.

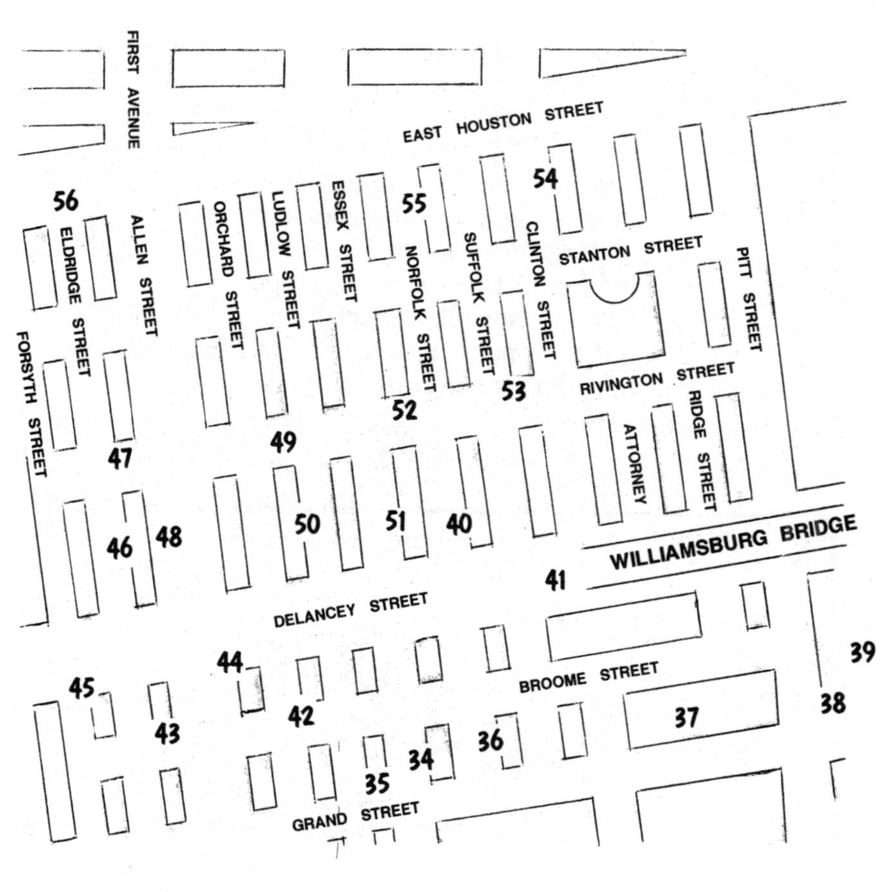

FIRST AVENUE
EAST HOUSTON STREET
56
ELDRIDGE STREET
ALLEN STREET
ORCHARD STREET
LUDLOW STREET
ESSEX STREET
NORFOLK STREET
SUFFOLK STREET
CLINTON STREET
STANTON STREET
PITT STREET
55
54
FORSYTH STREET
RIVINGTON STREET
RIDGE STREET
ATTORNEY
52
53
47
49
WILLIAMSBURG BRIDGE
46
48
50
51
40
41
DELANCEY STREET
44
39
45
BROOME STREET
38
43
42
37
36
35
34
GRAND STREET

STOP 40.   **LANSKY LOUNGE (RATNER'S)**
Norfolk Street (200 feet north of Delancey)
Tel. (212) 677-9489

The rear of Ratner's Restaurant used to be a "Speak Easy" during the Depression era. The back dining room of Ratner's has been converted into a jazz club and lounge for the local artist crowd of the Lower East Side and the East Village. It is named for the notorious gangster, Mayer Lansky.

The entrance to Lansky Lounge is via an underground alley. Look for a small spotlight and the name "Lansky" on the right side of Norfolk Street - directly opposite Ratner's parking lot. Or you can enter via the main restaurant entrance on Delancey Street.

STOP 41.   **WILLIAMSBURG BRIDGE**
East end of Delancey Street

The arrival of hundreds of thousands of East European Jews after 1900 and the razing of entire blocks of Lower East Side tenements to make way for the Williamsburg Bridge approach along Delancey Street in 1903, caused a great surge of Jewish migration over to Williamsburg, Brooklyn, directly across the East River.

The bridge, with its pedestrian ramps, trolley lines and subways, became a major link between the Jewish communities of the Lower East Side and Williamsburg.

STOP 42.   **LOWER EAST SIDE
TENEMENT MUSEUM**
90 Orchard Street   Tel. (212) 431-0233

"Tenement" is the term used to describe a five- or six-story walk-up apartment building. Many buildings of this style, designed for the masses of immigrants who came to New York City after the 1870s are located in the Lower East Side.

There are usually stores on either side of a central (metal) staircase. The entrance foyer is very narrow. A typical residential floor was originally designed to accommodate four small apartments. There were two toilets or water closets in the public corridor. Originally, there were no showers or baths in these "cold water flats." Some lucky immigrants would have a bathtub located in the kitchen, near the building's water lines. They would put a plank of wood over the tub, and voila, they would have a dining area!

Most immigrants, however, would go to the public bathhouses. The last public bathhouse in the Lower East Side was located at 133 Allen Street. That building was recently converted into an Oriental church. Today, all apartments in these old tenement buildings are required by law to have complete built-in bathrooms.

The central core of the tenement was required to have an air shaft. These air shafts often measured about two feet in depth. All rooms which required a window (bedroom, bathroom, etc.) often faced these dingy air shafts. The shape that these air shafts created in plan view, on both sides of each tenement, was a "dumbbell" shape, hence the term,"dumbbell" tenement.

So now, when you are looking at a continuous row of tenements, there are actually these air spaces (about four feet wide) between each building.

The Lower East Side Tenement Museum is located in a restored 1863 tenement on Orchard Street. The tour of the museum starts at 90 Orchard Street (corner Broome Street), where the visitor sees a short film in a mini-theater about the Lower East Side and its immigrant groups. The tour then proceeds across the street to #97 Orchard Street, where the visitors proceed to climb upstairs and view the restored tenement apartments, complete with turn of the century furniture and artifacts.

Diagonally across the street from the Lower East Side Tenement Museum gallery and ticket office (on Broome Street, between Orchard and Allen Streets), is the Lower East Side Tourist Information Center.

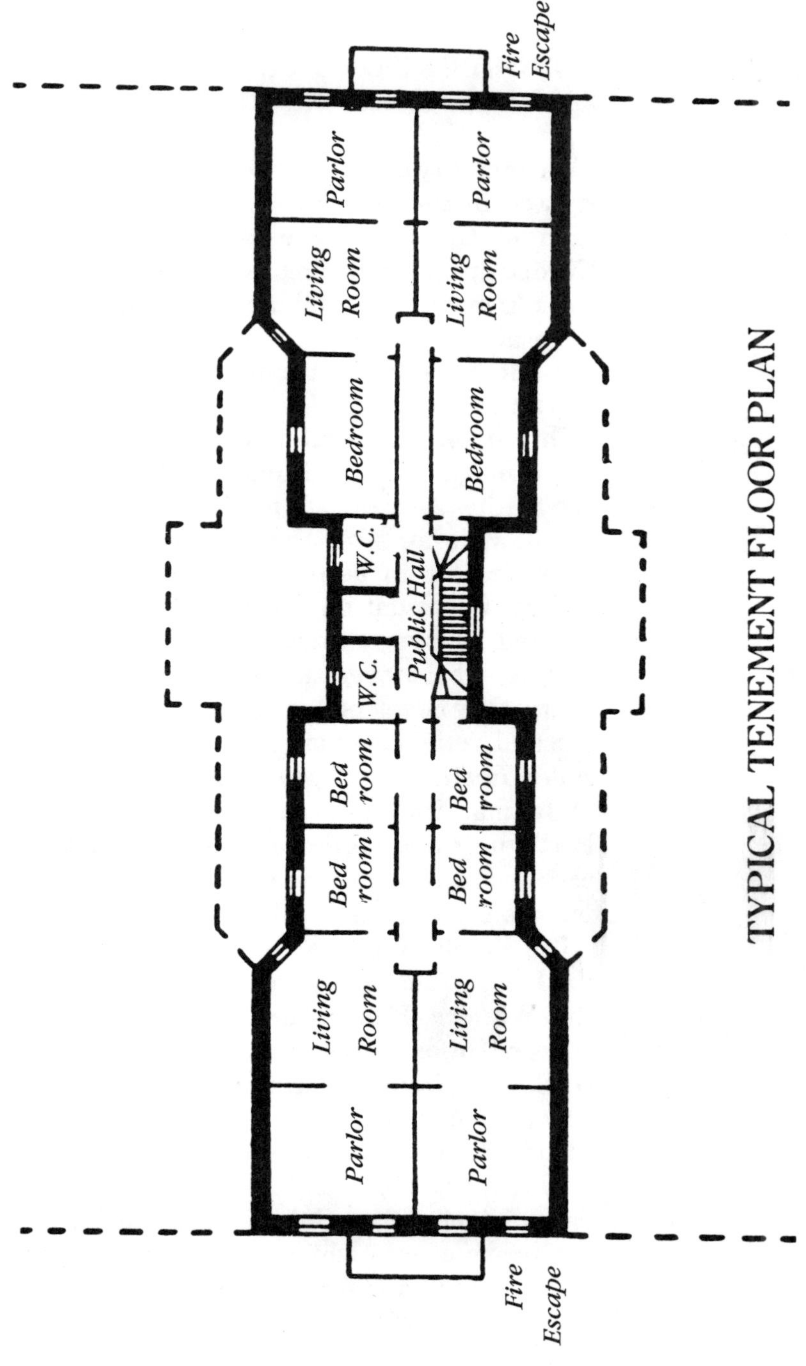
Fire Escape
Parlor
Parlor
Living Room
Living Room
Bedroom
Bedroom
W.C.
W.C.
Public Hall
Bed room
Bed room
Bed room
Bed room
Living Room
Living Room
Parlor
Parlor
Fire Escape
TYPICAL TENEMENT FLOOR PLAN

STOP 43.   **CONGREGATION JANINA**
280 Broome Street   Tel. (212) 431-1619

The majority of the Jewish immigrants who arrived in the Lower East Side around the turn of the century came from Eastern Europe and were fleeing the pogroms. These were known as the Ashkenazic Jews. There were also several groups who arrived from the Mediterranean countries. They were known as Sephardic Jews.

This small congregation on Broome Street has a magnificent and unique history. They are neither Ashkenazik nor Sephardic. They are Jews who, after the destruction of the Holy Temple in Jerusalem in the year 70 A.C.E., were sent on a slave ship to Rome. Instead, a storm forced them to land in Greece, where over the next two thousand years, they developed uniquely different ethnic and religious customs. This group was called *Romaniotes*. They settled in the town of Janina. They welcomed the Spanish and Portuguese (Sephardic) Jews after they were expelled from their respective countries during the Inquisition of 1492.

The Kehila Kedosha Janina Synagogue in the Lower East Side is the only synagogue in the Western Hemisphere of this tiny and obscure Greek Jewish community. There are weekly Sabbath services as well as on all Jewish holidays.

Upstairs in the womens' section is a beautiful exhibition of the history of the Jews of Janina, including a Holocaust Memorial and the tragic events which wiped out virtually 90% of Greek and Janina Jewry.

The congregation in New York was founded in 1906. The small synagogue is a replica of

Romaniote
Female Costume

Scroll
of Esther
(1890)

Torah from Janina, Greece

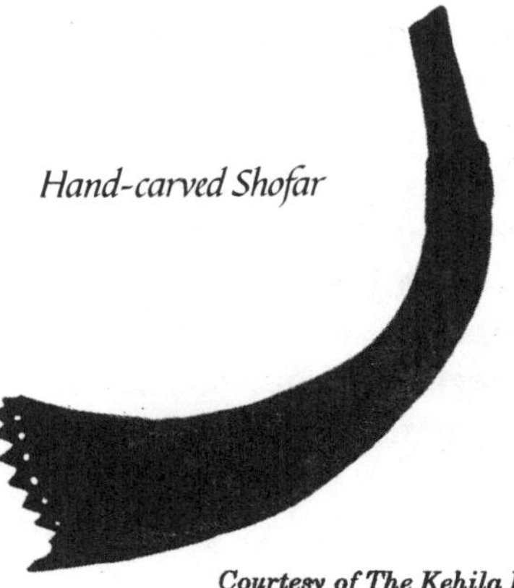

Hand-carved Shofar

Courtesy of The Kehila Kedosha Janina Synagogue and Museum

the one in Janina, Greece and was built in 1927. The synagogue is open on Sundays from 11:00 am to 4:00 pm or other times by reservation. Admission is by contribution.

STOP 44.

BANK OF THE UNITED STATES SITE
79 Delancey Street

This imposing structure was for many years the Bank of the United States. It was owned mostly by Jews and was believed to be an official institution of the United States Government, hence many of the Jewish immigrants invested their life savings in it. After the stock market crash of 1929, the bank fell upon hard times. When many of the major banks refused to grant the Bank of the United States short-term credit, many immigrants considered anti-Semitism to be the reason. The bank did actually fail in 1932, but most of the depositors were able to salvage most of their savings.

In the 1930s, the building was occupied by the Hebrew Publishing Company until the early 1980s. That company moved out to New Jersey.

STOP 45.

**UNION SQUARE
SEVENTH DAY ADVENTIST CHURCH**
128-130 Forsyth Street

On the southeast corner of Delancey and Forsyth Streets stands the Union Square Seventh Day Adventist Church. It was originally built as a synagogue in 1895 for Congregation Poel Zedek Anshe Ileya. The most fascinating feature in this building is along its Delancey Street façade. At the street level there were stores. These stores actually helped in the upkeep of the synagogue and then the church. In more recent times, there were Jewish shopkeepers in these stores paying rent to the church.

STOP 46. **UNIVERSITY SETTLEMENT HOUSE**
84 Eldridge Street

The University Settlement Society was organized in 1886. It was founded for the purpose of bringing men of education into closer relations with the laboring classes of the city, for mutual instruction and benefit. It aims to establish "settlements" in the tenement-house districts, where college men could carry out, or induce others to "carry out, all the reforms, domestic, industrial, educational, provident, or recreative, which the social ideal demands." The building still houses a community center.

STOP 47. **FORMER SYNAGOGUE**
58 Rivington Street

Congregation Adath Jeshurun of Jassy was organized in 1886 and built in 1903. The congregation later moved out and was replaced by the First Warsaw Congregation. That congregation disbanded as well. Several years ago, the building was purchased by a local artist.

STOP 48. **PUBLIC BATHS** (former)
133 Allen Street

The Tenement Reform Bill of April, 1901 prohibited the further construction of the "dumbbell" tenement. According to the new law, every residential building completed after January 1, 1902 had to allow for direct natural lighting of every room and to conform to such minimal health and safety standards as separate toilet facilities for each apartment and safely constructed fire escapes.

The immigrants who, unfortunately, had to live in the "old law" tenements would have to go to public bathhouses such as this one, located at 133 Allen Street, since their buildings did not have any shower or bath facilities.

This building was closed down by city health inspectors several years ago following the upsurge of the AIDS epidemic. Many homeless and "infected" people would come to this facility. It was therefore decided to close down the facility. The building was recently converted into a Chinese church.

The last public bath facility in the area has recently been restored. It is located on East 23rd Street, on the corner of Asser Levy Place, near the FDR Drive. Asser Levy was one of the original twenty-three Jews who arrived in New Amsterdam in 1654. The public bath facility was designed in 1906 by Arnold Brunner and William Martin Aiken.

Arnold Brunner was a noted architect who designed the present synagogue building for America's oldest congregation, Shearith Israel, in 1897. He also designed the Educational Alliance in the Lower East Side, Temple Beth El (Fifth Avenue & 76th Street), the West End Synagogue (166 West 82nd Street) and Temple Israel of Harlem (Lenox Avenue & 120th Street).

STOP 49.

THE ROUMANIASHE SHUL
89 Rivington Street   Tel. (212) 673-2835

Built as a Methodist church in 1888, the building was purchased just a few years after construction by Congregation Shaarey Shomayim, also known as the First Roumanian-American Congregation, but lovingly known as the *Roumaniashe Shul* by the locals.

The voices of such world-class cantors as Yossele Rosenblatt, Moshe Kousevitzky, Moishe Oysher, Jan Peerce and his brother-in-law, Richard Tucker resounded through the hallowed halls of the 1200 seat synagogue. The Roumaniashe Shul has been called the *Cantors' Carnegie Hall.*

There are daily services at 8 am and at 5 pm, primarily serving the local merchants, as well as on the Sabbath and the major Jewish holidays. The Romanesque Revival building has just undergone an exterior facelift, showing its original brick surface. Tours are available by prior arrangements. The small building to the left of the synagogue once housed the congregation's Talmud Torah.

STOP 50.

FORMER SYNAGOGUE
121 Ludlow Street

The main sanctuary of this former synagogue is now used as a warehouse. Chevrah Kadisha Anshei Sochechov was housed in this remodeled tenement in the 1920s.

STOP 51.

ESSEX STREET MARKET
Essex Street,
between Broome and Stanton Streets

For many of the newly-arrived immigrants around the turn of the century, the sweatshops were the only places where these unskilled laborers could find jobs. The working conditions were intolerable, not only because of the overcrowding and filth but also because they had to work twelve to sixteen hours a day, seven days a week, including Saturday, the Jewish Sabbath. A sign posted on the wall of the sweatshop stated quite simply, "If you don't come in to work on Saturday, don't bother coming in on Sunday!"

Many immigrants continued to work on the Sabbath since they had no other way of supporting their large families. Others went into business for themselves. They rented pushcarts and made their own "business hours." The streets were filled with these pushcarts, selling everything from rags *(shmat'es)* to buttons and thread. Orchard Street was a major artery for these pushcarts.

In the early 1930s, the city banned all pushcarts from Orchard Street, declaring that they were a major fire hazard–fire trucks could not pass through the pushcart-congested street. At that time, the Essex Street Market was constructed. It was designed to house all of the outlawed pushcarts from Orchard Street.

The Market has, over the years, become dilapidated and run down. Part of the Essex Street Market, near Stanton Street, has recently been converted into a local medical center.

STOP 52. **SCHAPIRO'S KOSHER WINERY**
124 Rivington Street   Tel. (212) 674-4404

Founded in 1899, Schapiro's Kosher Wines still uses the original oak vats in their cellar. The cellar actually continues under the sidewalks of Rivington Street. Kosher wine means that the processing of the wines are under rabbinical supervision. All of Schapiro's wines are processed in upstate New York and are *mevushal* (cooked), which is another step in the kashruth process.

During the Depression years, Schapiro's was permitted to operate since its product was for sacramental (religious) use.

Tours and wine tasting in the only kosher winery in Manhattan are available on Sundays or by appointment.

STOP 53. **STREITS MATZOH FACTORY**
150 Rivington Street   Tel. (212) 475-7000

The only matzoh factory in Manhattan is located at the corner of Rivington and Suffolk Streets. Tour of the facilities are no longer available due to insurance company restrictions. However, it is possible to purchase fresh products in the small store which carries Streits products. You can look into the factory and still see the modern machinery with conveyer belts carrying consolidated sheets of matzoh before they are broken into squares and packed into boxes.

STOP 54. **CONGREGATION CHASAM SOPHER**
8 Clinton Street   Tel. (212) 777-5140

Chasam Sopher is housed in the 1853 building designed for Rodeph Sholom.

This is the second oldest synagogue structure in New York City. It was built in 1853 for Congregation Rodef Shalom. That congregation is still functioning and is located on the Upper West Side at 7 West 83rd Street. Congregation Chasam Sopher purchased the building in 1891. The Orthodox Congregation Chasam Sopher is assisted in its upkeep and maintenance by its Reform predecessor, Rodef Shalom. Rodef Shalom feels it still has a link to its roots in the Lower East Side.

STOP 55.   **OLDEST SYNAGOGUE BUILDING**
172 Norfolk Street

Ansche Chesed was organized in 1828 by German Jews. It built this lavish Gothic Revival synagogue in 1849. It was designed by architect Alexander Saeltzer. It had a seating capacity of 1500. In 1874, the first congregation moved out and was replaced by Congregation Ohab Zedek. That second congregation moved to Harlem and is presently located on Manhattan's Upper West Side. The building was taken over in 1921 by Congregation Anshe Slonim. That congregation began to dwindle after World War II.

By 1975, the building stood abandoned and was slated for demolition. However, in 1986 the building was purchased at auction by a Spanish Jewish artist, Angel Orensanz, for $500,000. He now uses the lofty space of the main sanctuary as his studio and gallery.

STOP 56.   **SUNSHINE THEATER** (former)
147 Houston Street

This building was built ca. 1910 as the

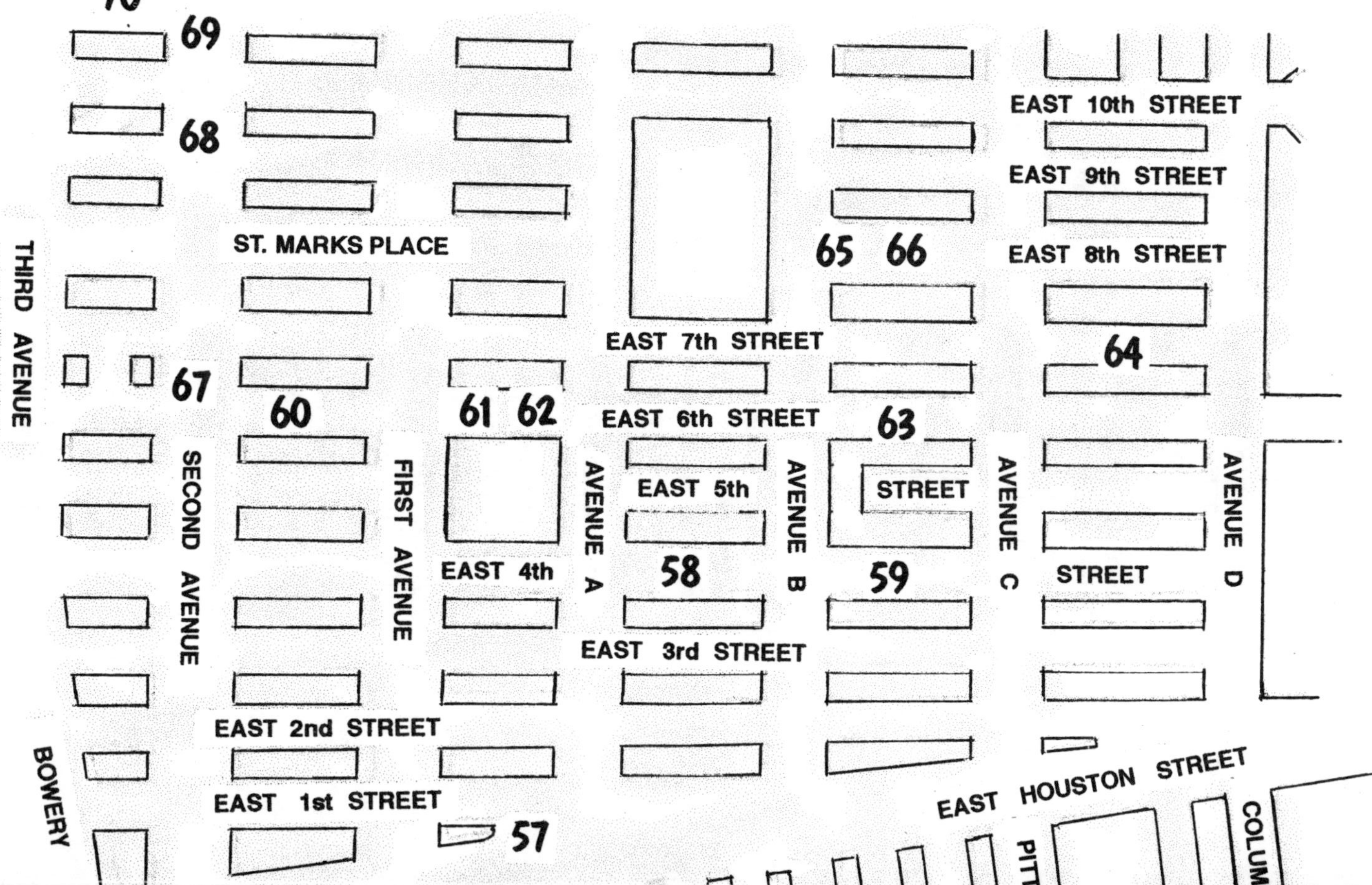

70
69
68
67
60
61 62
65 66
63
64
58
59
57
THIRD AVENUE
SECOND AVENUE
FIRST AVENUE
AVENUE A
AVENUE B
AVENUE C
AVENUE D
ST. MARKS PLACE
EAST 10th STREET
EAST 9th STREET
EAST 8th STREET
EAST 7th STREET
EAST 6th STREET
EAST 5th
EAST 4th
EAST 3rd STREET
EAST 2nd STREET
EAST 1st STREET
STREET
BOWERY
EAST HOUSTON STREET
PITT
COLUMB

Sunshine Theater. There were plans to renovate the building into a cafe and club.

STOP 57.   **FORMER SYNAGOGUE**
108 East 1st Street

Congregation Masas Benjamin Anshe Podhajce was an active congregation until the 1970s. Some young members in the community tried to keep the minyan going as long as they could. But in the late 1980s, the congregation folded. The tenement-style synagogue had a magnificent bimah reminiscent of a medieval Polish shtetl synagogue.

The building was taken over by a group which held concerts and poetry readings. It was known as "Synagogue Space." In recent years, the building has been turned into residential spaces.

STOP 58.   **FORMER SYNAGOGUE**
256 East 4th Street

STOP 59.   **FORMER SYNAGOGUE**
289 East 4th Street

This building housed Congregation Nachlath Zvi B'nai Israel Linath Hazedek B'nai Menashe in the 1920s.

STOP 60.   **COMMUNITY SYNAGOGUE CENTER**
325 East 6th Street   Tel. (212) 473-3665

Built in 1848 for the United German Lutheran Church. The church group went on an outing to the Bear Mountains in the late 1930s but met with disaster. The boat which the church group was sailing on capsized, drowning the entire congregation.

In 1940, the Community Synagogue purchased the former church building.

STOP 61. **CONGREGATION AYDUS YISROEL ANSHEI MEZRICH**
415 East 6th Street

This small synagogue, designed in Classic Revival style, was organized in 1892 and built in 1910. It is still functioning.

STOP 62. **FORMER SYNAGOGUE**
431 East 6th Street

The Center of the Proskurove Zion Congregation has been converted into a residential apartment building.

STOP 63. **FORMER SYNAGOGUE**
638 East 6th Street

This was the site of Congregation Ahavath Jeshurun Shaare Torah. The building on the right may have been used as the congregation's Hebrew school. But each building may also have been separate synagogues at one time.

STOP 64. **SYNAGOGUE CONDOS**
242 East 7th Street

The Beth Hamedrash Hagadol Anshe Ungarin was organized in 1883. The congregation designed this lovely Classic Revival synagogue in 1905. It was recently renovated and turned into condominiums.

The former synagogue at 242 East 7th Street has been converted into condominiums.

STOP 65.　**EAST SIDE HEBREW INSTITUTE** (former)
Avenue B and East 8th Street

This was one of several major Hebrew schools or yeshivas in the Lower East Side. It was built before World War I. In the 1960s, this area was in decline. It was known as "Alphabet City" (named so because of the street names–Avenue A, B, C, and D). Tompkins Square Park was the site of one of the city's major drug trafficking areas.

In recent years, however, things were improved. The police cleared the park of the drug addicts, the old bombed-out former tenement buildings were torn down or renovated and new "in-fill" housing was constructed. There are now outdoor cafes opposite the park. The former East Side Hebrew Institute building was abandoned for many years but has also been renovated. There are now residential apartments in the old building. The original name entablature, *Talmud Torah Darchei Noam*, is still visible. It was organized in 1916 and built in 1926.

STOP 66.　**EIGHTH STREET SYNAGOGUE**
317 East 8th Street　Tel. (212) 529-7557

This building once housed two separate congregations–Congregation B'nai Moses Joseph and Congregation Chevra Lecheth Yosher B'nai Horwitz. In recent years, the building was literally falling apart. Several local Jews are now in the process of stabilizing and restoring the old shul. The congregation is now called the Eighth Street Shul. There are special educational programs and concerts presented by the small community-oriented congregation.

STOP 67. **YIDDISH THEATER DISTRICT**
Second Avenue–
from East 4th to East 12th Streets

Second Avenue was once the "Jewish Rialto" of the Yiddish Theater. Classic plays as well as special productions were presented in Yiddish, the *Mother Tongue* of the majority of the Jewish immigrants who came to America around the turn of the century. They longed for the *Old Country* and many of these plays featured tales of life in the shtetls.

Among the remaining Yiddish theater buildings still standing are the Yiddish Art Theater, once known as the Eden Theater (now the Enter Media Theater) at East 12th Street; the Anderson Yiddish Theater at East 4th Street (now abandoned); and the Orpheum, at St. Marks Place.

STOP 68. **YIDDISH THEATER STARS' WALK**
156 Second Avenue

In front of the Second Avenue Deli is the Jewish version of Growmen's Chinese Theater with its Hollywood star-studded sidewalk. Some of the stars along Second Avenue include Molly Picon, Ben Bonus and the Barry Sisters. The sign in front of the deli reads, "This star-studded sidewalk was created to immortalize the great actors, actresses and musicians who graced the stages of the eight Yiddish theaters that once flourished along Second Avenue." There is another sign in the window of the deli which states, "The French have Cassoulet, we have Cholent."

The Second Avenue Deli serves kosher meats but is open seven days a week. A few years ago, the owner of the Second Avenue Deli, who was loved by everyone in the neighborhood, was gunned down while depositing the days' receipts in the bank.

STOP 69.　**HOME OF PETER STUYVESANT**
Second Avenue and East 10th Street

Peter Stuyvesant's mansion once stood on the site of St. Mark's-in-the-Bowery Church. Stuyvesant was the notoriously anti-Semitic Governor of New Amsterdam who greeted the first Jewish settlers in 1654. He put them in jail until orders were received from headquarters of the Dutch West India Company in Amsterdam, Holland. Many of the shareholders in that company were Jewish. They applied pressure on Peter Stuyvesant who ultimately permitted the 23 Jewish immigrants to live freely in the colony on the provision that they not be a "burden on the society."

The graveyard, containing Stuyvesant's vault, is now remodeled in undulating cobblestones and is used as a playground.

STOP 70.　**HEBREW TECHNICAL SCHOOL SITE**
26-36 East 10th Street

Founded in 1884, the Hebrew Technical School was a non-sectarian school. It was one of the first technical high schools in the United States. Its last graduating class was in 1939.

The school was conceived at a meeting of the United Hebrew Charities, the Hebrew Orphan Asylum and the Hebrew Free School Association for the purpose of training youths of immigrants in industrial arts. The building has been declared an official historic landmark and is presently part of New York University.

STOP 71.   **JOSEPH PAPP'S PUBLIC THEATER**
425 Lafayette Street   Tel. (212) 598-7100

The Hebrew Immigrant Aid Society (HIAS) was organized in the 1880s and furnished lawyers and interpreters to help the Jewish immigrants through the red tape of Ellis Island Immigration Station. They provided kosher food for steerage passengers who had not eaten any cooked meals since leaving the shtetls in the *Old Country*. They also provided temporary housing and employment information.

The HIAS headquarters was located in this building. It was originally built in 1853 as the Astor Library. It was designed by Alexander Saeltzer (architect of New York City's oldest synagogue structure, Ansche Chesed, located at 172 Norfolk Street, in the Lower East Side). The Astor Library later became part of today's New York Public Library at Fifth Avenue and 42nd Street.

In the late 1960s, the Romanesque Revival building was converted into seven indoor theaters for Joseph Papp's New York Shakespeare Festival. The complex was designed by Giorgio Cavaglieri. The first performance of the great rock musical *Hair* opened in this theater. *A Chorus Line* was also first premiered in this theater. During the summer months, the New York Shakespeare Festival offers free productions in its Central Park theatre-in-the round (near 81st Street). The Joseph Papp's Public Theater has been declared a National Historic Landmark.

STOP 72. **TRIANGLE FIRE SITE**
Washington Place & Greene Street

A bronze plaque at the northwest corner of Washington Place and Greene Street (just east of Washington Square Park in Greenwich Village) refers to the site of the Triangle Shirtwaist Company fire, a tragedy which took 143 lives, mostly young women, on the Saturday afternoon of March 25, 1911. The Loft Building which stands today on this corner, originally called the Asch Building, is the very building in which that holocaust took place.

The Triangle Company occupied the upper three floors of the ten-story structure. The owner of that sweatshop refused to let his workers go for coffee breaks, so he locked the doors to the factory–from the outside. When fire did break out, the young women couldn't open the exit doors and were forced to jump out the windows!

Following the fire, new and more stringent child-labor laws were instituted. State legislation provided for factory fire prevention and building inspection, sanitary working conditions, workmen's compensation and liability insurance, and shortened hours of labor for women and children.

The Triangle Fire took the lives of 143 young girls in 1911.

This building is part of the New York University campus.

STOP 73. **HEBREW UNION COLLEGE**
One West 4th Street   Tel. (212) 674-5300

In 1922, Stephen S. Wise founded the Jewish Institute of Religion in New York to provide training "for the Jewish ministry, research, and community service." Rabbi Wise was its president until 1948. The school was located adjacent to his Free Synagogue at 30 West 68th Street, in the Upper West Side until its present building was completed in 1980. The Jewish Institute of Religion merged with the Hebrew Institute of Religion (whose main campus is in Cincinnati, Ohio) in 1950.

The College prepares its students for the pulpit in congregations belonging to the Reform Movement. The Hebrew Union College presents lecture programs and museum exhibitions which are open to the general public.

The Old
Synagogues

The following list of over five hundred Lower East Side congregations was compiled in 1921. Most of these congregations are no longer in existance. Sometimes five or more small congregations were housed in one tenement building. The list is in alphabetical order by address.

Many of the congregations were named after the cities or small villages (shtetls) that were left behind in Eastern Europe. During the Holocaust, all of these Jewish communities were destroyed. The names of these congregations in this book now serve as memorials to those lost Jewish communities.

LOWER EAST SIDE SYNAGOGUES (by address)

78 Allen Street **Anshei Selib**
78 Allen Street **Ohel Jacob Chevrah Kadisha**
128 Allen Street **Tifereth Israel**
165 Allen Street **Fannie Siegel Anshei Berlader**
165 Allen Street **Tiphereth Israel Anshei Stepenesht**
192 Allen Street **Ajutarul Bukarester Handwerker Congregation**
9 Attorney Street **Khal Chasidim**
43 Attorney Street **Independent Achim mi'Makower**
48 Attorney Street **Khal Chasidim Anshei Razan**
50 Attorney Street **Adath Jeshurun Anshe Kamenetz**
86 Attorney Street **Jaroslower Kehilah**
86 Attorney Street **Oxyner Family Independent Kehilah**
86 Attorney Street **Trembovler First Kehilah**
87 Attorney Street **First Galician Congregation**
87 Attorney Street **Dukler Mugain Abraham**
88 Attorney Street **Dunajaver First Congregation**
93 Attorney Street **Buishtiner Chevrah Linath Hazedek Anshei Galicia**
93 Attorney Street **Vladover Slovotticher Gemilath Chasodim Verein**
99 Attorney Street **Adath Israel Anshei Galicia**
99 Attorney Street **Ansche Sfard**
99 Attorney Street **Oestreicher Ungarn Anshei Sfard**
102 Attorney Street **Chasidei Sadigera Tiphereth Israel Marisin**
102 Attorney Street **Karatchiner Rubin Chevrah**
137 Attorney Street **Stropkover Chevrah Joseph Chaim**
147 Attorney Street **Chevrah Help of Israel Anshei Ranizow**
149 Attorney Street **Chevrah Chasidei B'nai Israel mi'Rizin**
149 Attorney Street **Rhonishover Kehilah**
150 Attorney Street **Lemberger First Chevrah Anshei Ashkenaz**
161 Attorney Street **Chelmer Erste Congregation**
163 Attorney Street **Yavorower Erste Kehilah**
17 Avenue A **Chatimer Bessarabier Congregation**
17 Avenue A **Jagolniczer Kehilah**
28 Avenue A **Chevrah B'nai Menachem Anshei Horvetz**
28 Avenue A **Shaarei Avoda Lodge**
28 Avenue A **Sons of Solomon Anshe Jezierna**
22 Avenue C **Chevrah Ahavath Jonathan B'nai Jacob Anshei Pecheich**
90 Avenue C **Tiphereth Israel Anshei Sphard Galicia**
106 Avenue C **Ez Chaim Anshei Hungary**
155 Avenue C **Chevrah Anshei Narowla**
6 Avenue D **Brith Sholom B'nai Isaac**
8 Avenue D **Rava Ruska Congregation**
10 Avenue D **Krakowitzer Kehilah**
48 Avenue D **Ahavath Abraham B'nai Kolo**
136 Avenue D **Ohavei Emeth**
31 East Broadway **Ohavay Sholom**

44 East Broadway Anshe Emes (B'nai Emeth Maryompoler)
49 East Broadway Matte Levi
68 East Broadway Chevrah Anshei Oshmineh v'Anshei Trab
87 East Broadway B'nai Israel Anshei Kaidan
98 East Broadway Agudath Achim Anshei Kusnitza
98 East Broadway Yeshibath Rabenu Mordechai Rosenblatt
103 East Broadway Ahavath Achim Anshe Usda
103 East Broadway Ahavath Torah
147 East Broadway Beth Abraham Anshei Trestina
147 East Broadway Chevrah Anshei Devin
147 East Broadway Chevrah Anshei Mir
147 East Broadway Talmud Torah Tiphereth Jerusalem
183 East Broadway United Hebrew Community - Adath Israel
190 East Broadway Lenas Hazedek
197 East Broadway People's Synagogue
198 East Broadway Young Israel Synagogue
203 East Broadway Adath Israel
206 East Broadway Ahavath Achim d'Mohilev
206 East Broadway Chevrah Ohel Jacob Anshei Dubna
206 East Broadway Orberik Chevrah
206 East Broadway Scherpser Chevrah
209 East Broadway Chevrah B'nai Menachem
209 East Broadway Chevrah Etz Chaim Anshei Ruzian
209 East Broadway Chevrah Midrash Anshei Schenedeva
214 East Broadway Hebrew League
225 East Broadway Anshei Panedel
225 East Broadway Shaarei Bino
227 East Broadway Beth Haknesseth Proshnitzer Anshei Poland
227 East Broadway Chevrah Adath Kdoshim Anshei Rozinol
227 East Broadway Chevrah Rabenu Nachum Anshei Grodno
227 East Broadway Chevrah Rodfei Zedek Anshei Ritova
227 East Broadway Chevrah Tifereth Israel Anshei Kraulover
246 East Broadway Bikur Cholim Anshei Bialystok
264 East Broadway Ansia Prelock
142 Broome Street Downtown Talmud Torah Institute
201 Broome Street Beth Haknesseth Anshei Lubavitz v'Homler
232 Broome Street Chevrah Ahavath Zedek Anshe Jaskinover
232 Broome Street Jeshofisar Chevrah
236 Broome Street Chevrah Sphard Anshei Poland
269 Broome Street Mishnaioth Chasidei Trisk Umikarev
280 Broome Street Congregation Janina
48 Cannon Street Lutawisker First Chevrah Machzikei Hadath
62 Cannon Street Austrian-Hungarian Anshei Sphard
100 Cannon Street Gemilath Chesed Kehilah
24 Chrystie Street Beth Hamedrash Shaarei Torah
24 Chrystie Street B'nai Israel Salanter Anshe Samut
56 Chrystie Street Kol Israel Ansche Suwalk
186 Chrystie Street Brotherhood League of Rhodes (Agudath Achim d'Rhodes)
10 Clinton Street Rodef Sholom
10 Clinton Street Chasam Sopher
66 Clinton Street Chevrah Massoth Benjamin Anshei Pohaja

The oldest synagogue structure in the city is located at 172 Norfolk Street. It was built in 1849.

67 Clinton Street Tlumaczer Congregation
80 Clinton Street B'nai Moses
80 Clinton Street Czortkover Rabbi J.M. Shapiro Kehilah
80 Clinton Street First Linath Hazedek Anshei Potokzlotz
82 Clinton Street Praskwerer Zion Congregation
90 Clinton Street B'nai Lippner Ahavath Israel
90 Clinton Street Chernustroff Verein
90 Clinton Street Linath Hazedek Anshei Sadikoff
90 Clinton Street Sedagarer Lutzker
90 Clinton Street Yaslovitzer Verein
96 Clinton Street B'nai David Anshei Charshel & Yanova
96 Clinton Street B'nai Jacob Anshei Chechonowze
96 Clinton Street Hoaredenker Erste Congregation
151 Clinton Street New Peoples' Congregation
169 Clinton Street Chevrah T'hilim Anshei Viscover
180 Clinton Street Mogen Abraham Anshei Ostrolimo
225 Clinton Street Beth David Anshei Rakov
225 Clinton Street Chevrah B'nai Israel Anshei Lamzitze
53 Columbia Street Zmigroder Congregation Benjamin Joseph
65 Columbia Street Anshei Gliniany
66 Columbia Street Anshei Socol Belz
66 Columbia Street Bikur Cholim Anshei Zormin
66 Columbia Street Tarngroder Benevolent Association
70 Columbia Street Ahavath Achim Anshe Hungary
80 Columbia Street Koreth Brith Anshei Sphard
81 Columbia Street B'nai Samuel Levenson Congregation
81 Columbia Street Madliborzger First Congregation
81 Columbia Street Mazel Bosetz
81 Columbia Street Radimer Congregation B'nai Mordechai Menachem
81 Columbia Street Tiphereth Joseph Anshei Przemsyl
88 Columbia Street Linsker Erste Chevrah Bikur Cholim
90 Columbia Street Christonopoler Congregation B'rith Isaac
90 Columbia Street Jarychzover Independent Young Men's
                                          Benevolent Association

90 Columbia Street Kreshover Kehilah
90 Columbia Street Rabbi Meyer Parmishlauer
                                  Sick & Benevolent Association
90 Columbia Street Shoboshiner Independent Congregation
90 Columbia Street Tamashower Congregation
92 Columbia Street Dombromiler First Kehilah
92 Columbia Street Anshei Krashnik Lubliner Gubernia
92 Columbia Street Frampoler Erste Kehilah
92 Columbia Street Shendishower Galizianer Erste Congregation
120 Columbia Street Beth Hemedrash Shearith Israel
122 Columbia Street Agudath Bachurei Chemed
122 Columbia Street Bolochover Chevrah Shomrei Sholom
122 Columbia Street Erste Chevrah Ahawath Israel Anshei Larea
130 Columbia Street Lantzer Verein
138 Columbia Street Baligrader Chevrah Agudath Chaverim
140 Columbia Street NysanderDembizer Chevrah
                                  Machneh Reuben B'nai Aaron

178 Delancey Street Chevrah Kadisha Levy mi'Barditshov
203 Division Street B'nai Simon Solomon Congregation
203 Division Street Shomrei Sabbath Anshei Lebovner Wohliner
237 Division Street Khal Chasidim Anshei Kuronitz
245 Division Street Ahavath Zedek B'nai Lebedowe
245 Division Street Gemilath Chasodim Anshe Motele
277 Division Street Shem Tov Anshei Janover
30 East 1st Street Czortkover Rabbi D.M. Friedman Congregation
108 East 1st Street Chevrah Agudath Achim Anshei Mishwitz
108 East 1st Street Masas Benjamin Anshei Podhajce
193 East 2nd Street Zalisczicker Rabenu Ager Erste Verein
207 East 2nd Street Uscrechker First Kehilah
209 East 2nd Street Anshe Dubiner
209 East 2nd Street Broder First B'nai B'rith Association
209 East 2nd Street Katriner Congregation
214 East 2nd Street Anshei Achim Elizabethgrader
214 East 2nd Street Borochauer Chevrah
214 East 2nd Street Galician Chevrah Freedman
214 East 2nd Street Mikulinzer First Independent
Sick Benevolent Association
214 East 2nd Street Sushover Chevrah
214 East 2nd Street Telchan Seventewaler
214 East 2nd Street Washkowitzer Bukowinian
First Sick Benevolent Society
214 East 2nd Street Yad Charutzim Monesterzisker
214 East 2nd Street Yednitzer Chevrah
241 East 2nd Street Shaarei Tphillah Anshei Doliner
218 East 2nd Street Rymalover Kehilah B'nai Jacob
254 East 2nd Street Rohatyner Young Men's Society
223 East 2nd Street Buczaczar First Chevrah
65 East 3rd Street Chochmath Adam mi'Plinsk Independent Chevrah
291 East 3rd Street Anshe Dushikower Galicia
293 East 3rd Street Chevrah B'nai Israel
308 East 3rd Street Moshcisker Chevrah Gur Arye
388 East 3rd Street Zion Congregation Talmud Torah of Manhattan
297 East 3rd Street Chevrah Bachurim Anshe Ungarn
62 East 4th Street Dorshei Tov Anshei Ottynia
66 East 4th Street Kishinever First Congregation
85 East 4th Street Lodzer Chevrah Agudath Achim
87 East 4th Street Shomer Sabbath
257 East 4th Street Anshei Novisielitzer Bessarabia
261 East 4th Street B'nai Sholom
255 East 4th Street Chevrah Shaarei Torah Anshei Hungary
281 East 4th Street M'vasereth Zion
289 East 4th Street Nachlath Zvi B'nai Israel Linath Hazedek B'nai Menasheh
316 East 4th Street B'nai Peyser
341 East 4th Street Talmud Torah Beth Machsh l'Yesomim Anshei Zitomer
372 East 4th Street Anshei Mielitz
622 East 5th Street Chevrah Kadisha Talmud Torah
622 East 5th Street Kolbuszower Teitelbaum Congregation
B'nai Chaim Machneh Reuben

630 East 5th Street B'nee Sholom
630 East 5th Street Chevrah Bikur Cholim B'nai Israel Anshei Baranov
415 East 6th Street Adath Israel Anshei Mizrach
431 East 6th Street Center of the Progressive Zion Congregation
636 East 6th Street Anshei Mozir
638 East 6th Street Ahavath Jeshurun Shaare Torah
638 East 6th Street Shearith B'nai Israel
804 East 6th Street Ohel Torah Talmud Torah
207 East 7th Street B'nai Rappaport Anshei Dumbrowa
242 East 7th Street Beth Hamedrash Hagadol Anshe Ungarin
317 East 8th Street B'nai Moses Joseph
317 East 8th Street Chevrah Lecheth Yosher B'nai Horwitz
East 8th & Avenue B East Side Hebrew Institute
228 East 10th Street Tenth Street Congregation
349 East 10th Street Anshei Petrikow
375 East 10th Street Anshei Chasidei Vishnitze Austria
132 East 11th Street Shearith Israel mi'Turkey Kehilah Kedosha
673 East 11th Street Chevrah Adath Zvi Yehudah
327 East 13th Street Talmud Torah Tiphereth Israel
241 East 14th Street Kol Adath Israel
216 East 15th Street Shaar Shomoyim
12 Eldridge Street Beth Haknesseth Kapolier
16 Eldridge Street Khal Adath Jeshurun and Anshei Lubz
83 Eldridge Street Chevrah Zichru Torath Moshe
87 Eldridge Street Chevrah Achei Grodno v'Anshei Staputkin
87 Eldridge Street Tifereth Jeshurun
133 Eldridge Street Agudath Achim Aram Zobah
133 Eldridge Street Chevrah Balter Society
133 Eldridge Street Chevrah B'nai Moshe Anshei Neesta Chechonavitz
133 Eldridge Street Chevrah Rodfei Sholom Anshei Polutzk
133 Eldridge Street Hatika Bessarabia Erste Kehilah
133 Eldridge Street Ostrer First Oheb Sholom
175 Eldridge Street Agudas Achim Anshe Kurland
175 Eldridge Street B'nai Jacob David Anshei Wishograd
193 Eldridge Street Chevrah Achei Joseph
9 Essex Street Chevrah B'nai Kodesh Anshei Kroz
100 Essex Street Dorshei Tov Dobroczynshe
131 Essex Street Chevrah Ahavath Achim Anshei Bilsk
20 Forsyth Street Kol Israel Anshei Poland
22 Forsyth Street Chevrah Dorshei Tov Anshei Pinsk
27 Forsyth Street Mishkan Israel Suwalki
80 Forsyth Street Beth Hamedrash Shaarei Torah
                           & Anshei Ratzk u'Matte Levi
85 Forsyth Street Agudath Achim Y'lidei Roumania
85 Forsyth Street Dorshei Zedek Anshei Kriutz
86 Forsyth Street Chevrah B'nai Hashvotim Anshei Novgorod
98 Forsyth Street Ahavath Sholom Monastir
98 Forsyth Street Ahavath v'Achvath Janina
98 Forsyth Street Bethlehem Judah B'nai Resitze
98 Forsyth Street Chevrah Ara Roschra
98 Forsyth Street Tiphereth Achim
106 Forsyth Street American Minsker Gemilath Chesed

Holy Ark detail in the Bialystoker Synagogue.

106 Forsyth Street Malener Chevrah
106 Forsyth Street Odesser Congregation
123 Forsyth Street Nachal Isaac Dorshei Tov
126 Forsyth Street Beth Haknesseth Poalei Zedek Anshei Ileya
144 Goerck Street Sokolover First Congregation Anshei Yosher
153 Goerck Street Rabbi Solomon Shapiro Anshei Minkacs
40 Gouveneur Street Anshei Lefler
40 Gouveneur Street Anshei Shzedriner
40 Gouveneur Street Menachem Zion Nusach Ari
311 Grand Street Smargona Chevra Kadisha
311 Grand Street Wohlin Chevrah Anshei Malzer
380 Grand Street Chevrah Tiphereth Achim Anshei Sirotsk
380 Grand Street Eliezer Damasek Congregation
385 Grand Street Beth Hamedrash Hagadol d'Sphardim
385 Grand Street Cochav Jacob Anshei Kamenitz d'Lita
387 Grand Street Luborner Wohliner Verein
410 Grand Street Chevrah Beth Chasidim d'Poland
436 Grand Street Chesed l'Abraham Anshei Trisk
38 Henry Street Chaari Zedek
85 Henry Street Ohavei Sholom
85 Henry Street Toldoth Isaac Nusach Sphard
89 Henry Street Ahavath Zedek Anshe Timkowitz
89 Henry Street Chave Boysim Anshe Minsk
89 Henry Street Progressive Brothers of Neshives
97 Henry Street Chai'ei Adam Anshei Minsk
135 Henry Street Chevrah Mishkan Anshei Zetel
136 Henry Street B'nai Pithechei Teshuva Anshe Anikst
136 Henry Street Chevrah Anshei Alt Konstantin
156 Henry Street Agudas Anshe Mamud u'Bais Vaad Lachachomim
156 Henry Street Minsker Old Men's Benevolent Association
156 Henry Street Pocccchavitzer Congregation
161 Henry Street Degel Machaneh Israel
165 Henry Street Memorial Rabbi Jacob Joseph
169 Henry Street Beth Abraham Chasidim d'Slonim
169 Henry Street Chasidei Libawitz
169 Henry Street Chevrah Sphard Anshei Pereyaslow
184 Henry Street Chevre Anshe Babroyska
184 Henry Street Chevrah Nusach Ho'ari
184 Henry Street Mishkan Israel Anshei Pruzina
184 Henry Street Zemach Zedek Nusach Ari
193 Henry Street Adath Jacob Anshei Slabodke
193 Henry Street Linath Hazedek Anshei Sakolka
197 Henry Street Anshei Torath Chesed
197 Henry Street B'nai Aaron Solomon Chevrah Anshei T'hilim mi'Govrove
197 Henry Street Chevrah B'nai Joshua Anshei Telz
197 Henry Street Tiphereth Achim Anshei Dunaberg
203 Henry Street Anshei Bobruisk
203 Henry Street Anshei Meakover of Polen
203 Henry Street Jeshuath Jacob Anshei Horadezer
203 Henry Street Kosher Butcher Retailers' Independent Association
203 Henry Street Yeshiva Rabbi Jacob Joseph

217 Henry Street B'nai Isaac Anshe Lechowitz
240 Henry Street Chevrah Anshei Stuchin & Grayewa
240 Henry Street P'eir Israel Anshei Yodnovner
295 Henry Street Chevrah Beth Hillel
9 Hester Street Beth Elijah
9 Hester Street Ostrover Congregation
21 Hester Street B'nai Jeshurun Anshei Kolni
23 Hester Street Chochmath Adam Anshei Lomza v'Gotch
38 Hester Street Talmud Torah
55 Hester Street Knesseth Israel
67 Hester Street Rote Toe Shelim
70 Hester Street First Roumanian Congregation
85 Hester Street Beth Hamedrash Beth Isaac
85 Hester Street Chevre Anshei Zimbrova
92 Hester Street Ahavath Sholom Anshe Winetza
93 Hester Street B'nai Isaac Anshe Lechowitz
99 Hester Street Oheb Sholom Anshei Charny
101 Hester Street Chai'ei Adam Anshei Lomza
101 Hester Street Chevrah Anshei Nevarodok
105 Hester Street Chevrah Agudath Achim Anshei Pesk
174 East Houston Street Jassy Roumanian Bohusher Congregation
228 East Houston Street Buczaczer Congregation
258 East Houston Street Choroshower Kehilah
328 East Houston Street B'nai Benjamin Moses Anshei Bolechow
328 East Houston Street Glogauer Verbruderungs Verein
435 East Houston Street B'nai Joseph Anshei Rymanow
436 East Houston Street Chevrah B'nai Aryei Judah
438 East Houston Street Mardiher Chevrah B'nai Zion
438 East Houston Street Kolbushover B'nai Levi
33 Jefferson Street Chevrah Anshei Sholom Kaidenow
56 Lewis Street Anshei Ulanov and Umgegend
69 Lewis Street Chevrah Kadisha Ez Chaim
84 Lewis Street Anshei Yanov Lublensky
101 1/2 Lewis Street Gorlitzer Erste Congregation Machzikei Emeth
102 Lewis Street B'nai Moses Joseph Anshei Zasmer & Zaviethast
105 Lewis Street Dubetzker Erste Congregation
115 Lewis Street Mosaski Chevrah Gur Arye
117 Lewis Street Bluziver Chevrah Degel Machnei Ephraim
126 Lewis Street B'nai Mordechai Moses Zvi
15 Ludlow Street B'nai Israel Anshei Piontnitza
15 Ludlow Street Chevrah B'nai Abraham Anshei Oretshe
27 Ludlow Street Aaron David Anshei Lubitz
27 Ludlow Street B'nai Moses Chasidei Kobrin
63 Ludlow Street Drubniner Chevrah
73 Ludlow Street Duvesaver Erste Independent Congregation
121 Ludlow Street Chevrah Kadisha Anshei Sochetchov
159 Ludlow Street Agudath Achim Misdai Lovon
141 Madison Street Beth Aaron Anshei Kaidonov
148 Madison Street Chevrah Beth Aaron Chasidim d'Kaidonow
162 Madison Street Chevrah B'nai Siraier
162 Madison Street Chevrah Oheb Sholom Anshei Krinker

209 Madison Street   **Agudath Achim Anshei Barisoff**
209 Madison Street   **Ez Chaim Anshei Wolozin**
240 Madison Street   **B'nai Moses Anshei Jendzivo**
240 Madison Street   **Chevrah B'nai Abraham Samuel**
240 Madison Street   **Tiphereth Jerusalem**
260 Madison Street   **Chevrah B'nai Aryei Anshei Krasnople**
290 Madison Street   **Anshe Wilna**
320 Madison Street   **Chevrah Mishnaioth Anshei Berezin**
30 Market Street   **Chevrah Anshei Ivenitz**
37 Market Street   **Anshei Smorgin B'nai Chaim Abraham**
52 Market Street   **Chevrah Orach Chaim Anshei Radoshkowitz**
71 Monroe Street   **Chevrah B'nai Jacob Anshei Shatzk**
85 Monroe Street   **Achei Jacob Anshei Senier**
85 Monroe Street   **Chevrah Mishkan Israel**
115 Monroe Street   **Ezrath Anchim Anshei Vidz**
116 Monroe Street   **Kether Torah Kehal Chasidim Anshei Kurevitz**
122 Monroe Street   **Adath Israel**
142 Monroe Street   **Machzikei Harav**
162 Monroe Street   **Chevrah Shomrei Emunah Anshei Lubon**
238 Monroe Street   **Atereth Zkenim**
34 Montgomery Street   **Machzike Torah Aushar Sineer**
35 Montgomery Street   **Chevrah Beth Abraham Anshei Dalhiner**
63 Montgomery Street   **Beth Haknesseth Anshei Olshan v'Anshei Eveun**
30 Norfolk Street   **Chevrah T'hilim Anshei Sterenke**
30 Norfolk Street   **Gleigeshudler Verein**
30 Norfolk Street   **Russian Painters Benevolent Association**
30 Norfolk Street   **Shaarei Tphillah Anshei Kobrin**
54 Norfolk Street   **Beth Hamedrash Hagadol**
60 Norfolk Street   **Chevrah Mishnaioth Shomrei Sabbath**
80 Norfolk Street   **Agudath Achim Anshei Brisk d'Lita**
80 Norfolk Street   **Poltusker Congregation Anshei Poland**
119 Norfolk Street   **Agudath Achim Anshei Schwinziane**
119 Norfolk Street   **B'nai Rabbi Zindel Anshei Pultinsk**
119 Norfolk Street   **Yad Savel**
146 Norfolk Street   **Ohab Zedek**
172 Norfolk Street   **Anshe Slonim**
20 Orchard Street   **Sons of Jacob Anshei Tiktim**
26 Orchard Street   **Chevrah Agudath Beth Achim Anshei Stupitz**
26 Orchard Street   **Chevrah B'nai Aaron Anshei Vilkomir**
26 Orchard Street   **Chevra Rodfei Sholom**
26 Orchard Street   **Chevrah Rodfei Sholom Anshei Rubsevitz**
32 Orchard Street   **Anshe Zhitomer u'Lid**
32 Orchard Street   **Bikesh Sholom Anshei Ostrova**
36 Orchard Street   **Chevrah Tiphereth Achim Anshei Sphard**
48 Orchard Street   **Chevrah Ohavei Sholom Anshei Sokoley**
48 Orchard Street   **Meshbisher Verein**
48 Orchard Street   **Shaarei Zedek Chevrah**
52 Orchard Street   **Beth Haknesseth Sokolower**
52 Orchard Street   **Chevrah Ahavath Achim Anshei Bohoslow & Korson**
52 Orchard Street   **Chevrah Beth Aaron v'Yisrael Chasidei Stolin**
56 Orchard Street   **Nachelska Chevra Congregation**

The former First Warsaw Congregation on Rivington Street has been renovated as an artist's loft.

56 Orchard Street Umaner First Congregation
86 Orchard Street **Pride of the East** (Tifereth Mizrach)
119 Orchard Street **Shevet Achim Anshe Slonim**
217 Park Row **Chatham Jewish Center**
13-15 Pike Street **Sons of Israel Kalvarier**
28 Pike Street **Adath Israel Anshei Birz**
28 Pike Street **Adath Wolkowisk**
28 Pike Street **Chevrah Ahavath Achim Anshei Krasna**
28 Pike Street **Chevrah B'nai Abraham Samuel Ashisker**
28 Pike Street **Mariampoler B'nai Emeth Congregation**
34 Pike Street **Ahavath Achim Anshe Usda**
34 Pike Street **Beth Haknesseth Anshe Slutzk**
66 Pike Street **Beth Haknesseth Ahavath Zion**

15 Pitt Street **Ahavath Achim Anshei Rodomyz**
24 Pitt Street **Anshei Sedid**
24 Pitt Street **Oheb Israel Anshei Mezhibesh**
36 Pitt Street **Rabbi Meir Przemyzlower Independent Chevrah**
54 Pitt Street **Brith Solam**
54 Pitt Street **Agudath Achim mi'Krakow**
54 Pitt Street **Pol Zedek**
62 Pitt Street **Chevrah Agudath Achim Anshei Fishers**
62 Pitt Street **Chevrah B'nai Jacob Anshei Czernovey**
62 Pitt Street **Sondowa Wisznia First Society**
64 Pitt Street **Chasidei Bayon Anshei Russia**
64 Pitt Street **Zaliner Erste Chevrah**
80 Pitt Street **Achim v'Reim Anshei Bresdowitz**
26 Ridge Street **Sheveth Achim B'nai Levi Anshei Chromsch v'Gometz**
33 Ridge Street **Shomrei Hadath Anshei Chelm**
73 Ridge Street **B'nai Israel Anshei Zurow Galicia**
87 Ridge Street **Anshei Zolkiev Tvuath Shor**
87 Ridge Street **Busker B'nai B'rith**
87 Ridge Street **Chevrah m'Zudath Zion B'nai Joshua Chariff**
87 Ridge Street **Oestreicher First Chevrah B'nai Rabbi Moses Abbe**
89 Ridge Street **Machzike Hadath Anshei Zborow**
89 Ridge Street **Adath Israel**
110 Ridge Street **Linath Hazedek Anshei Rosdol**
118 Ridge Street **First Zolaszer Ahavath Achim Congregation**
118 Ridge Street **Zboraver First Congregation**
122 Ridge Street **Shniaver Anshei Sphard**
123 Ridge Street **Rikihover Agudath Achim**
125 Ridge Street **Am Kedoshim Anshei Bobrika**
145 Ridge Street **Przworsker Erste Anshei Frishtak**
159 Ridge Street **Machzikei Hadath Anshei Zlotshov**
148 Ridge Street **Eliezer Ganz & Independent Pzemizler Congregation**
58 Rivington Street **Adath Jeshurun of Jassy**
58 Rivington Street **First Warsaw Congregation**
81 Rivington Street **Chevrah Shearith Israel Bousher Stefineshter Kruz**
89 Rivington Street **First Roumanian-American Congregation**
(Shaarei Shomayim)
125 Rivington Street **Gwozdziecer Independent Congregation**
125 Rivington Street **Kaluszer Independent Kehilah**

Moshe Kousevitzky served as cantor of the Roumanyisha Shul on Rivington Street.

125 Rivington Street Kamionker Strumilawer Erste Kehilah
125 Rivington Street Kopitshinzer Erste Sick & Benevolent Association
125 Rivington Street Obertiner Erste Chevrah
126 Rivington Street First United Podhaycer Congregation
129 Rivington Street Pomizaner Lodge
134 Rivington Street First Zablotower Congregation
159 Rivington Street Delatiner Erste Congregation
159 Rivington Street Halitzer Erster Verein
159 Rivington Street Neustadter First Congregation
37 Rivington Street Chevrah B'nai Isaac Anshei Nariov
37 Rivington Street Erste Bobriker Kehilah
37 Rivington Street Chevrah Reim Ahuvim mi'Rhybeshow Anshei Poland
63 Rivingtpn Street First Chevrah Bikur Cholim Linath Hazedek
Rutgers Place Chevrah Mogen David Anshei Brok
9 Rutgers Place Mesilath Yeshorim
9 Rutgers Place M'vakshei Sholom Anshei Molodedzner
9 Rutgers Street Beth Jacob Anshei Rachfalovsky
9 Rutgers Street Gluboker Congregation
9 Rutgers Street Ner Tamid Anshei Lubashov
32 Rutgers Street Judah and Israel Chevrah
92 Rutgers Street Chevrah Beth Israel Anshei Hlusk
56 St. Marks Place Young Men's Educational League
57 St. Marks Place Radomer First Congregation
236 Second Avenue Cantors' Association Synagogue
45 Sheriff Street Oheb Sholom Anshei Bukatchatze
48 Sheriff Street Atereth Chaim Halberstam
49 Sheriff Street B'nai Jacob Joseph
49 Sheriff Street Rodfei Zedek Anshe Balshovtza
49 Sheriff Street Rozodover Congregation B'nai Moses Horowitz
71 Sheriff Street Achim Ahuvim
71 Sheriff Street Ahavath b'Nach
77 Sheriff Street Dzikover Erste Chevra
77 Sheriff Street Sanaker Congregation Shomrei Hadath
77 Sheriff Street Breziver Brook Erste
80 Stanton Street Botachaner First Congregation Or Chodosh
97 Stanton Street Beth David Anshei Roman Roumania
178 Stanton Street Erste Chevrah B'nai David Anshei Radimashe
178 Stanton Street Dinever Kehilah
179 Stanton Street Adath Morom
180 Stanton Street B'nai Jacob Anshe Brazazan
180 Stanton Street Kolomayer Independent Kehilah
180 Stanton Street Magrower Erste Kehilah
180 Stanton Street Nihaver Berhometh First Benevolent Kehilah
188 Stanton Street Ahavath Israel Anshei Sphard
272 Stanton Street Tiphereth Jacob Anshei Appalla
294 Stanton Street Baranower Erste Congregation
296 Stanton Street Atereth Judah Zvi mi'Stetin
337 Stanton Street Rudniker Erste Kehilah
11 Suffolk Street Anshei Yanover & Kablier
30 Suffolk Street Achim Zetomer Wolin

Pushcarts on the Lower East Side, circa 1900.
Museum of the City of New York

30 Suffolk Street   Moshe Joseph Chevrah
56 Suffolk Street   Agudath Achim Anshei Kupishok
56 Suffolk Street   Doresh Tov Dobzinsky
56 Suffolk Street   Chevrah Mogen David Anshei Charusch
56 Suffolk Street   Rodfei Zedek Anshei Bulioko
63 Suffolk Street   Chevrah Degel Isaac
71 Suffolk Street   Beth Haknesseth d'Chevrah Sphardim d'Poland
71 Suffolk Street   Kehilath Jacob Anshei Meseritch
155 Suffolk Street   Chordoromer Erster Verein
155 Suffolk Street   Ostiler First Aid Society
155 Suffolk Street   Rodeph Sholom Independent Podhirzer Chevrah
169 Suffolk Street   Chevrah Kadisha
169 Suffolk Street   Talmud Torah Anshei Poland
177 Suffolk Street   Rabbi Hillel Lichtenstein Congregation
7 Willett Street   Beth Haknesseth Anshei Bialystok
48 Willett Street   B'nai Rabbi Aryei Snshei Strelisk
52 Willett Street   Rabbi Samuel Nachum Independent Tishminitze Kehila
58 Willett Street   Jeshuat Jacob Anshei Krakow
62 Willett Street   First Congregation B'nai Rabbi David Mayer
                                             Anshei Schwirsh
70 Willett Street   Beth Hamedrash Hagadol Anshe Resha
70 Willett Street   Beth Hamedrash Hagadol Anshe Ungarin

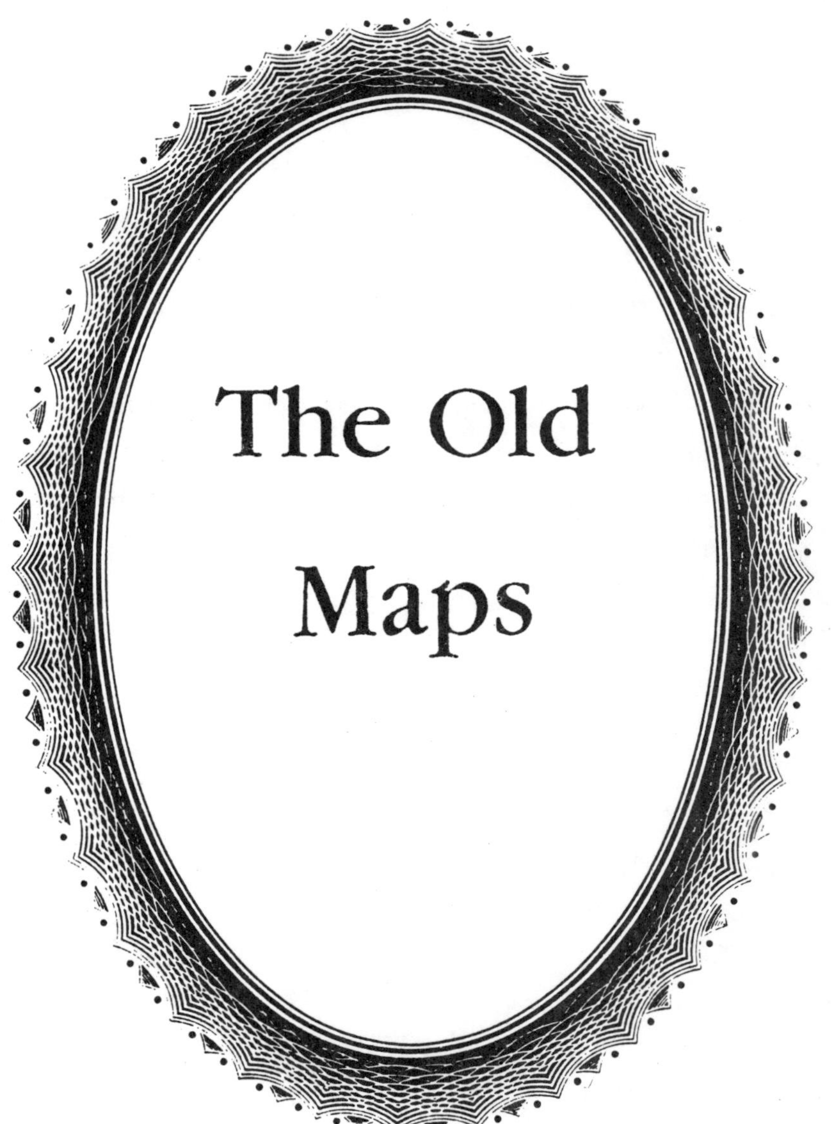
The Old
Maps

The following maps were taken from Bromley's *Atlas of Manhattan - 1914*. They contain every building which existed in the Lower East Side in that year. Many of the original streets such as Sheriff, Goerick and Cannon Streets were cleared following World War II to make room for the high-rise projects and Co-Ops. Occasionally, the original Dutch and English farm boundaries have been dotted in, e.g. around First Avenue and 6th Street.

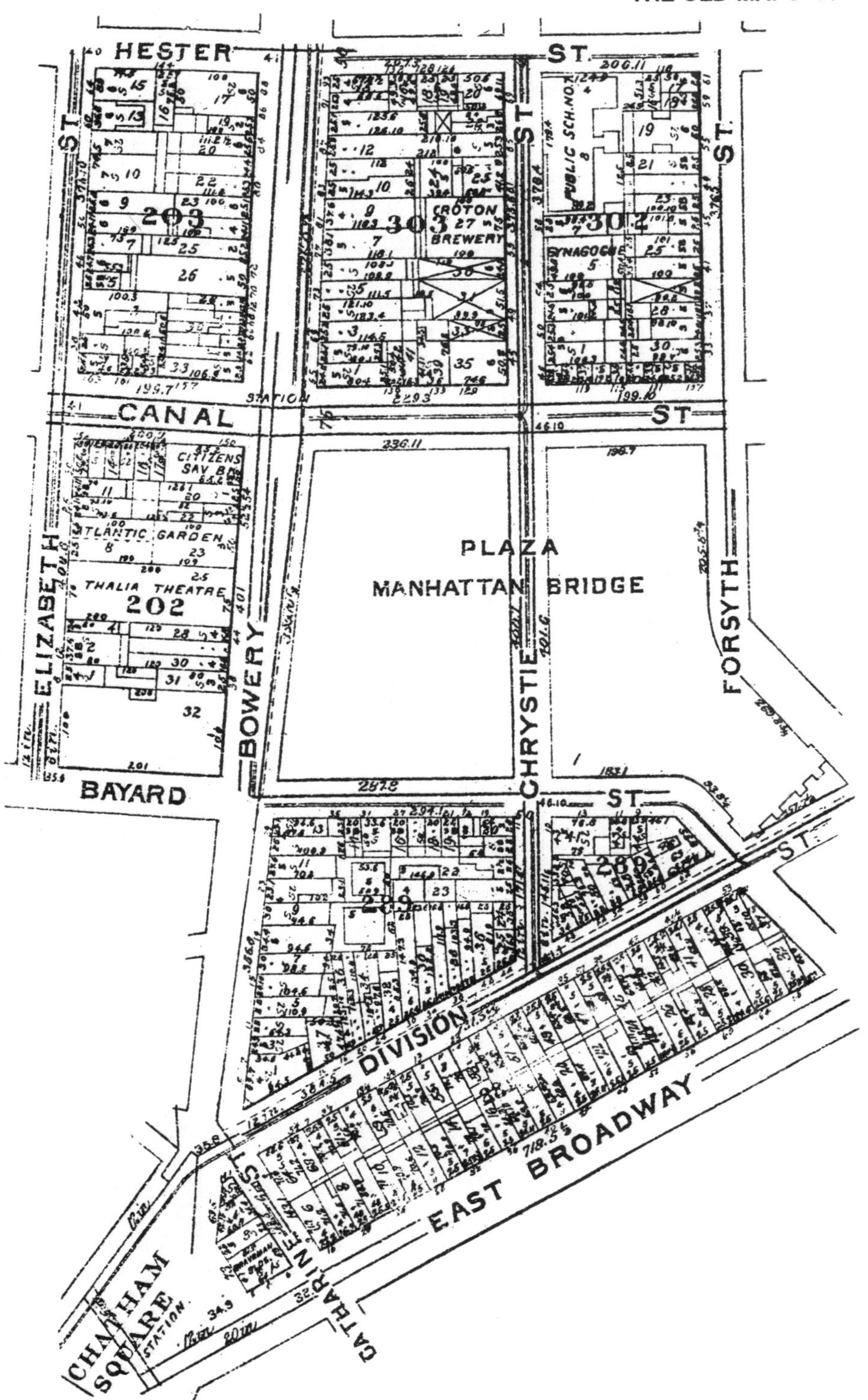
HESTER
ST.
ST.
ST.
ST.
ST.
ST.
PUBLIC SCH. NO. 1
CROTON
BREWERY
SYNAGOGUE
203
303
302
CANAL
STATION
ST.
CITIZENS
SAV. B'K
ATLANTIC GARDEN
THALIA THEATRE
202
ELIZABETH
BOWERY
PLAZA
MANHATTAN BRIDGE
CHRYSTIE
FORSYTH
BAYARD
ST.
289
299
DIVISION
CATHARINE
EAST BROADWAY
CHATHAM
SQUARE
STATION

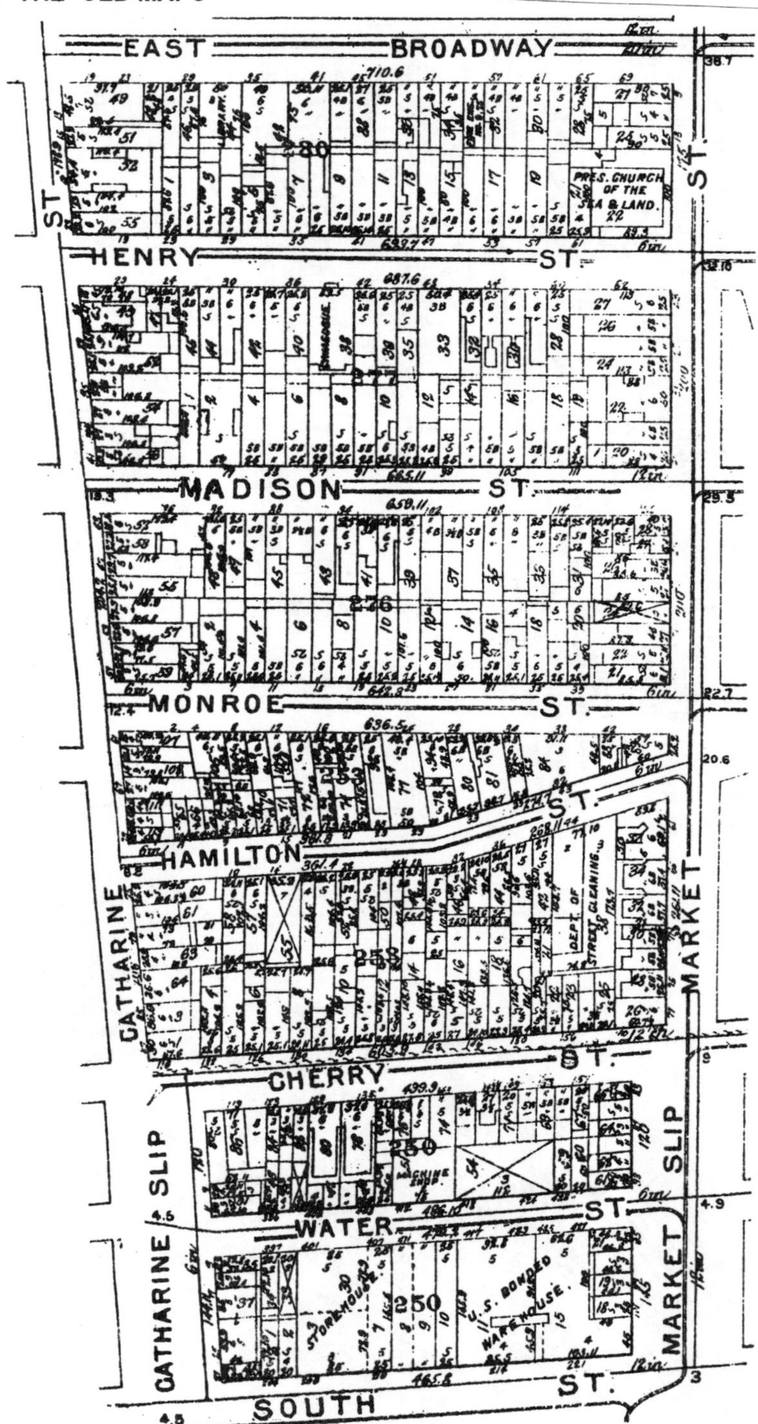

*The Third Avenue El linked the Jewish communities
of the Lower East Side, Harlem and The Bronx.*

Courtesy of the Merlis Collection

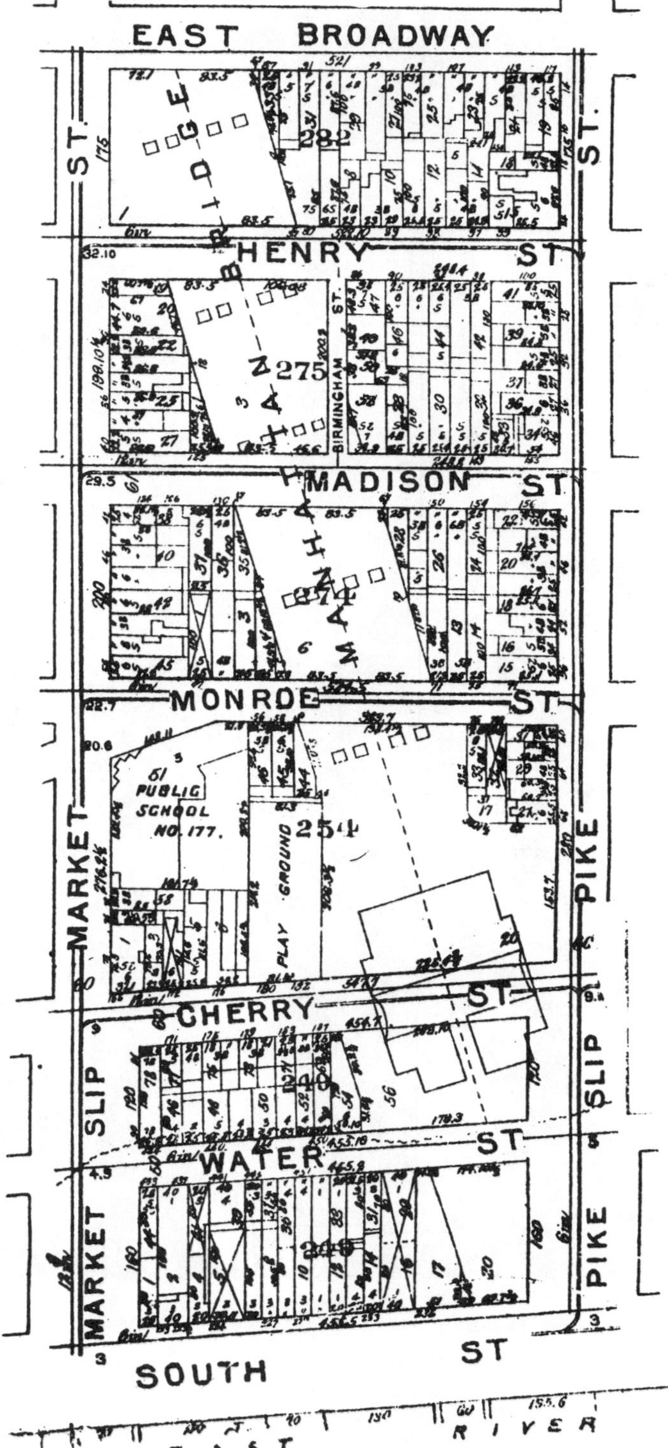
EAST BROADWAY
HENRY ST
MADISON ST
MONROE ST
CHERRY ST
WATER ST
SOUTH ST
EAST RIVER
MARKET ST
PIKE ST
MARKET SLIP
PIKE SLIP
PUBLIC SCHOOL NO. 177.
PLAY GROUND
BIRMINGHAM ST.
281
275
279
254
249
240

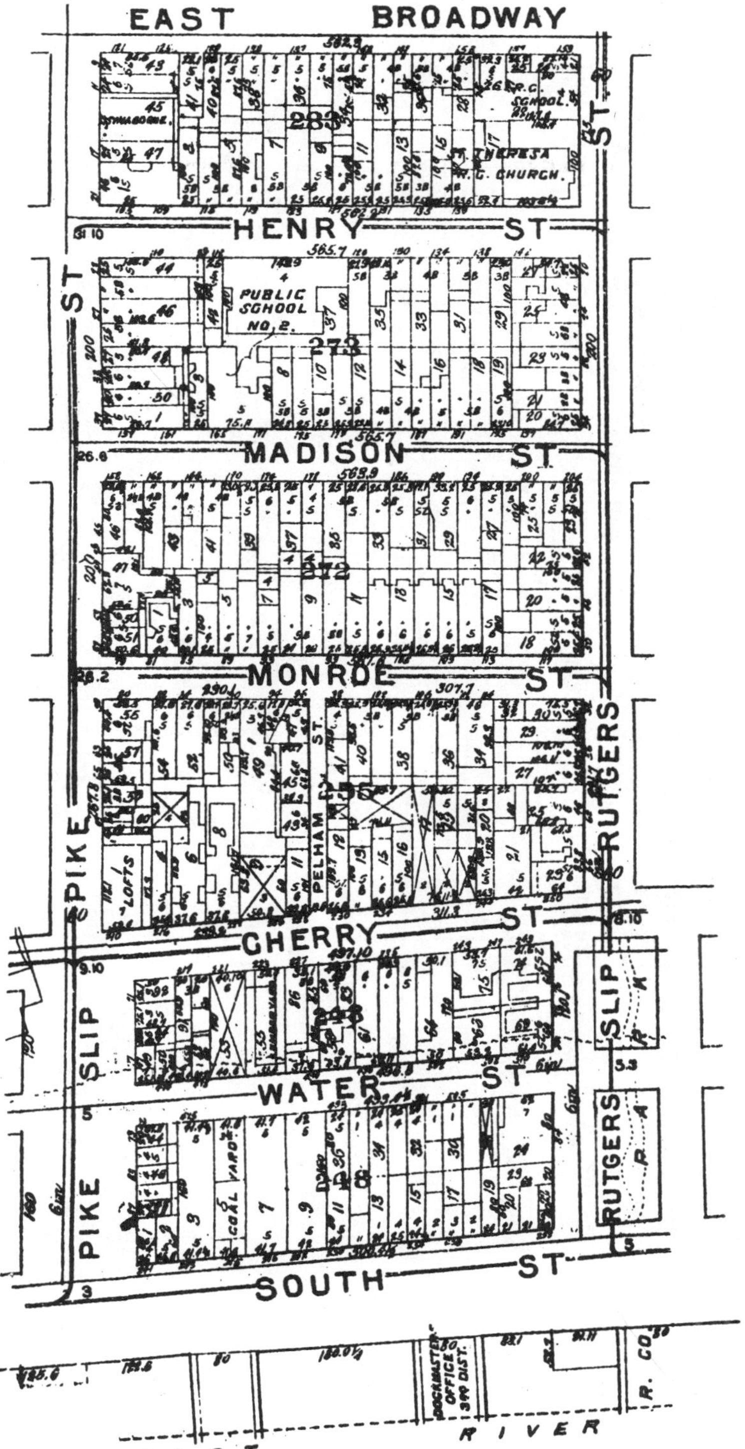

EAST BROADWAY
HENRY ST
MADISON ST
MONROE ST
CHERRY ST
WATER ST
SOUTH ST
PIKE ST
PIKE SLIP
RUTGERS ST
RUTGERS SLIP
SYNAGOGUE
PUBLIC SCHOOL NO. 2
ST. THERESA R.C. CHURCH
R.C. SCHOOL
PELHAM ST
LOFTS
COAL YARD
DOCKMASTER OFFICE 3RD DIST.
EAST RIVER
R. CO.

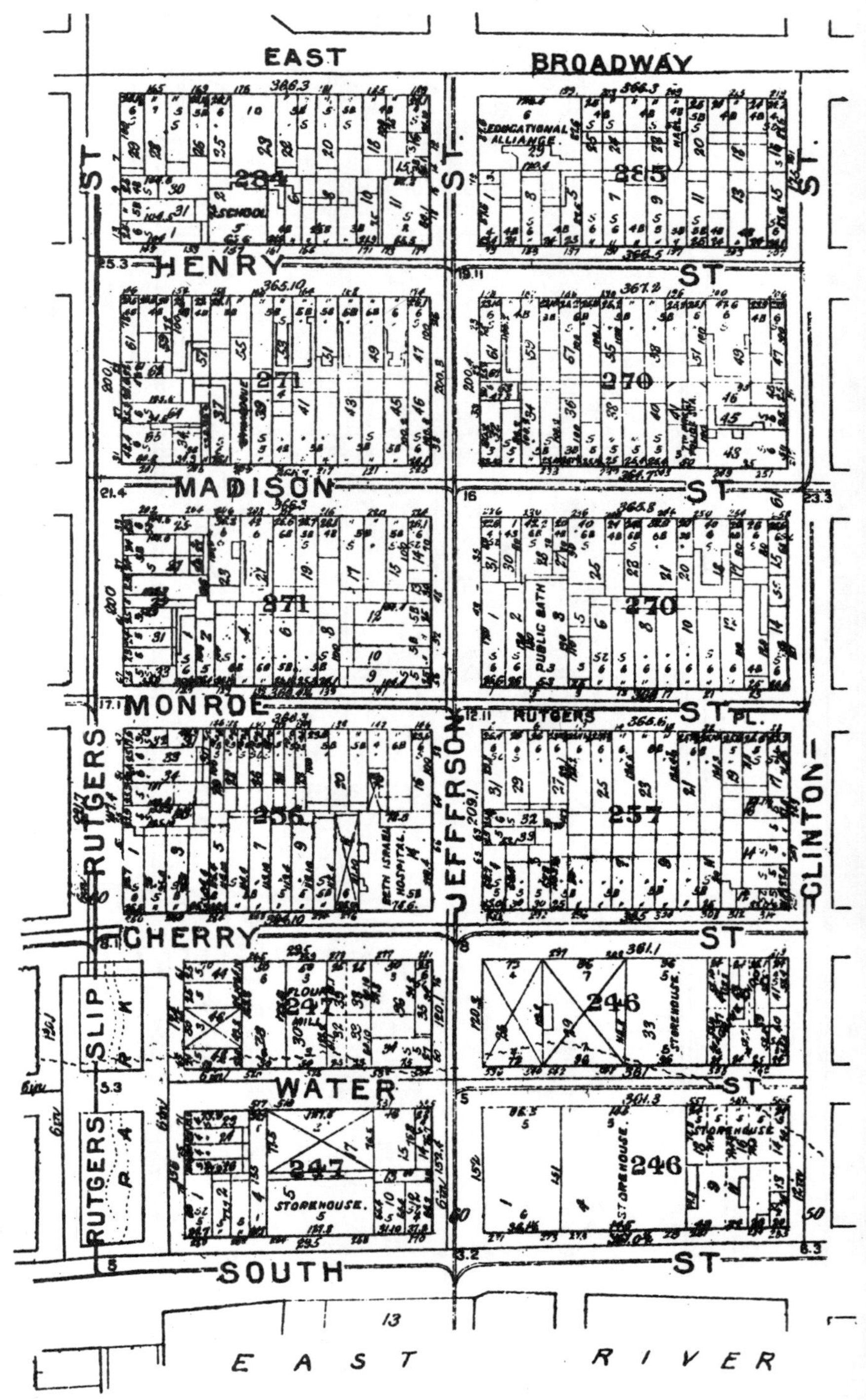

EAST   BROADWAY
ST
HENRY   ST
MADISON   ST
MONROE   RUTGERS   ST PL.
CHERRY   ST
WATER   ST
SOUTH   ST
EAST   RIVER
RUTGERS ST
JEFFERSON
CLINTON
RUTGERS SLIP
EDUCATIONAL ALLIANCE
PUBLIC BATH
BETH ISRAEL HOSPITAL
SCHOOL
FLOUR MILL
STOREHOUSE
STOREHOUSE

Third Avenue El, circa 1930.

Courtesy of the Merlis Collection

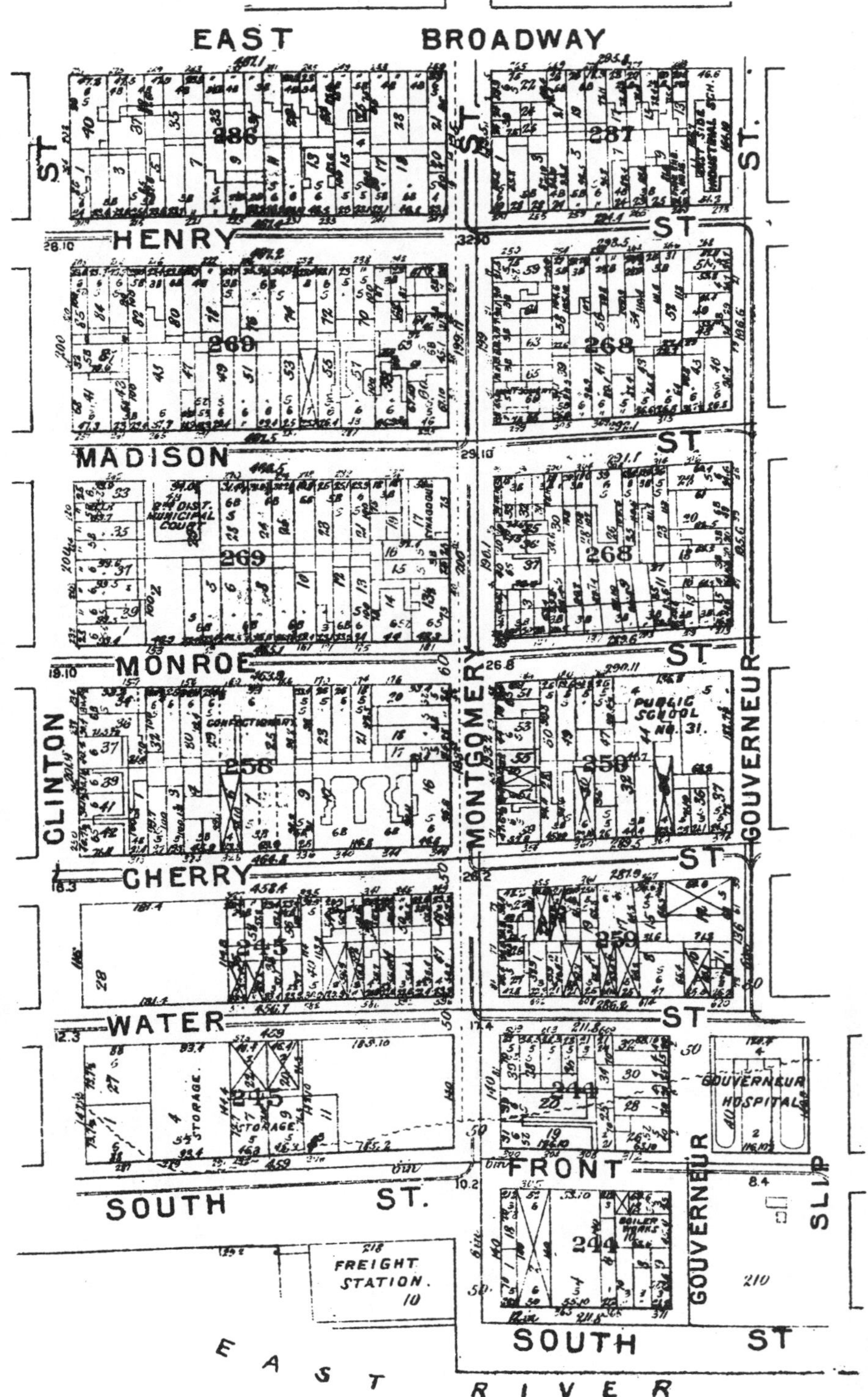
EAST BROADWAY
ST
ST
286
287
EAST SIDE INDUSTRIAL SCH.
HENRY
ST
269
268
MADISON
ST
2nd DIST. MUNICIPAL COURT
SYNAGOGUE
269
268
CLINTON
MONROE
ST
MONTGOMERY
PUBLIC SCHOOL NO. 31.
CONFECTIONERY
258
250
GOUVERNEUR
CHERRY
ST
259
WATER
ST
STORAGE
STORAGE
249
244
GOUVERNEUR HOSPITAL
FREIGHT STATION. 10
FRONT
BOILER HOUSE
244
GOUVERNEUR
SLIP
SOUTH ST.
SOUTH ST
EAST RIVER

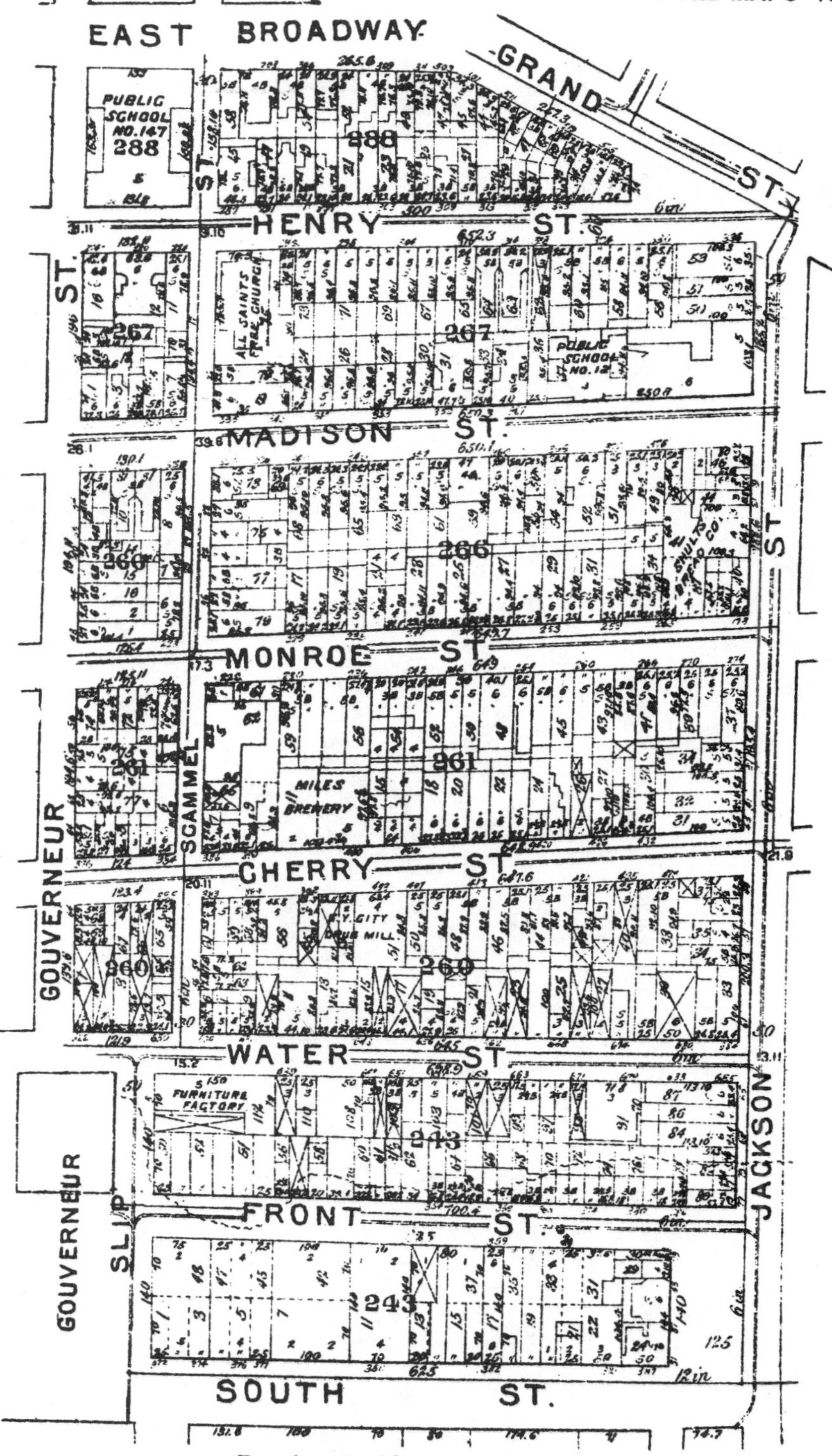
EAST BROADWAY
GRAND ST.
PUBLIC SCHOOL NO.147 288
HENRY ST.
ST.
267
ALL SAINTS FREE CHURCH
267
PUBLIC SCHOOL NO.12
MADISON ST.
266
266
MONROE ST.
261
MILES BREWERY
261
SCAMMEL
GOUVERNEUR
CHERRY ST.
N.Y. CITY DRUG MILL
260
260
WATER ST.
FURNITURE FACTORY
243
JACKSON ST.
FRONT ST.
243
GOUVERNEUR SLIP
SOUTH ST.
EAST RIVER

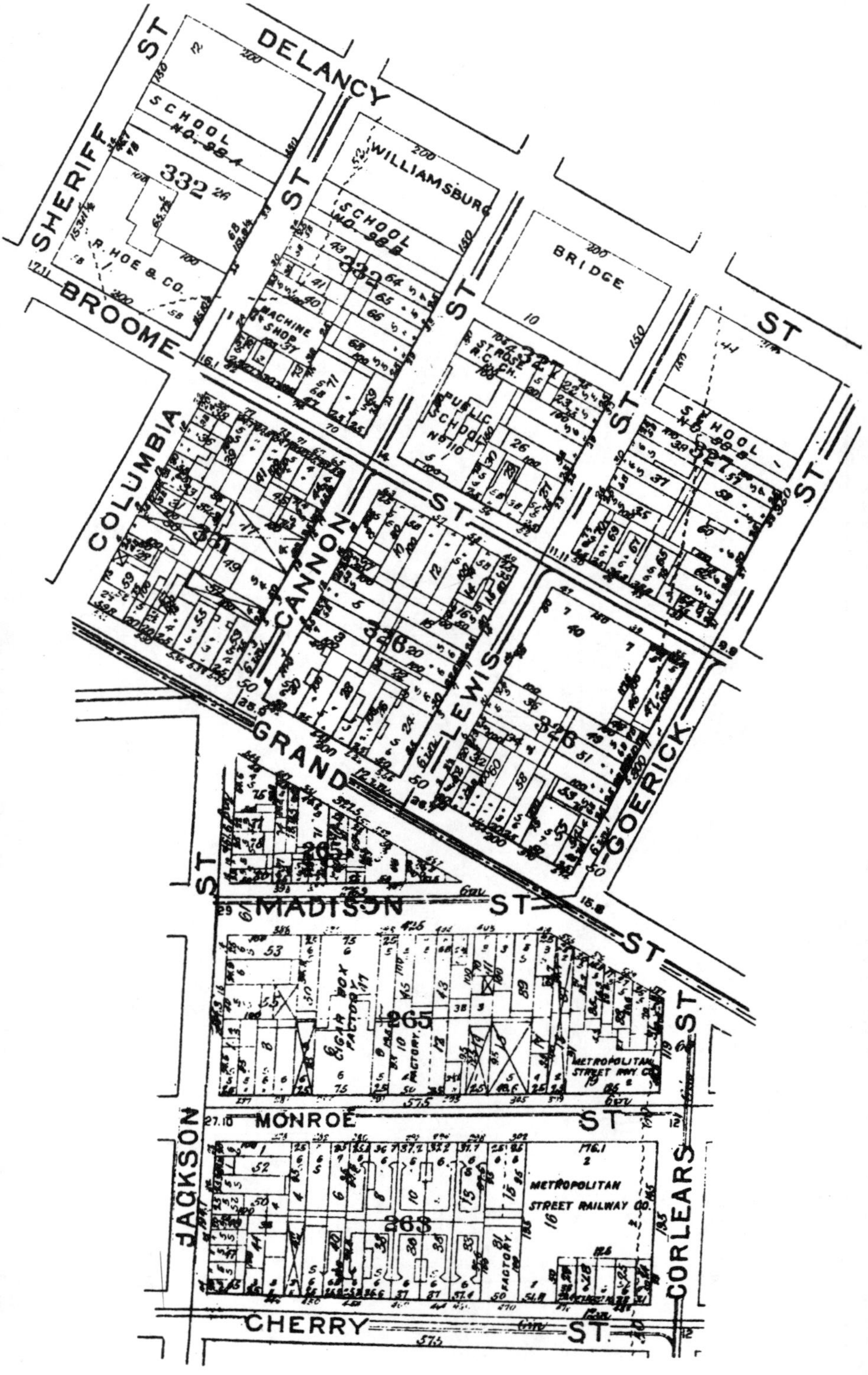

SHERIFF ST
DELANCY ST
BROOME ST
SCHOOL NO. 98 A
332
R. HOE & CO.
WILLIAMSBURG
SCHOOL NO. 98 B
ST
BRIDGE
ST
MACHINE SHOP
ST. ROSE R.C. CH.
PUBLIC SCHOOL NO. 110
SCHOOL NO. 98 B
COLUMBIA
CANNON
LEWIS
GOERICK
ST
GRAND
MADISON ST
265
EAGLE BOX FACTORY
METROPOLITAN STREET RWY CO.
JACKSON
MONROE ST
263
METROPOLITAN STREET RAILWAY CO.
FACTORY
CORLEARS
CHERRY ST

Courtesy of the Museum of the City of New York

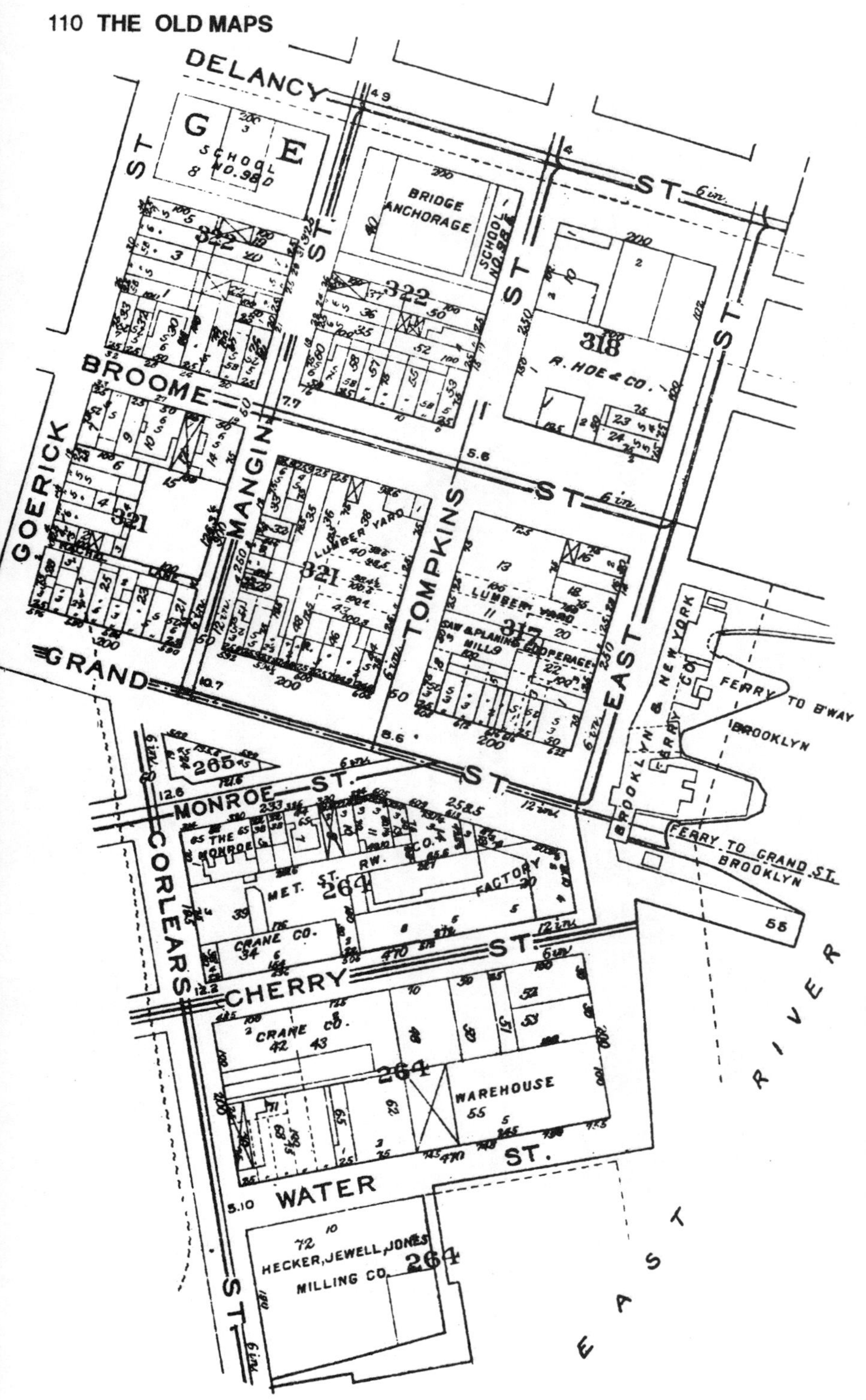
DELANCY
ST
G E
SCHOOL
NO.98
BRIDGE
ANCHORAGE
SCHOOL NO.98
ST
318
A. HOE & CO.
ST
BROOME
GOERICK
MANGIN
321
322
322
TOMPKINS
LUMBER YARD
321
ST
LUMBER YARD
317
SAW & PLANING MILLS
COOPERAGE
EAST
BROOKLYN & NEW YORK FERRY CO
FERRY TO B'WAY
BROOKLYN
GRAND
265
ST
MONROE ST.
THE MONROE
MET. ST. RW.
264
FACTORY
FERRY TO GRAND ST.
BROOKLYN
CORLEARS
CRANE CO.
34
CHERRY
ST
CRANE CO.
42   43
264
WAREHOUSE
55
RIVER
WATER
HECKER, JEWELL JONES
MILLING CO. 264
EAST
ST

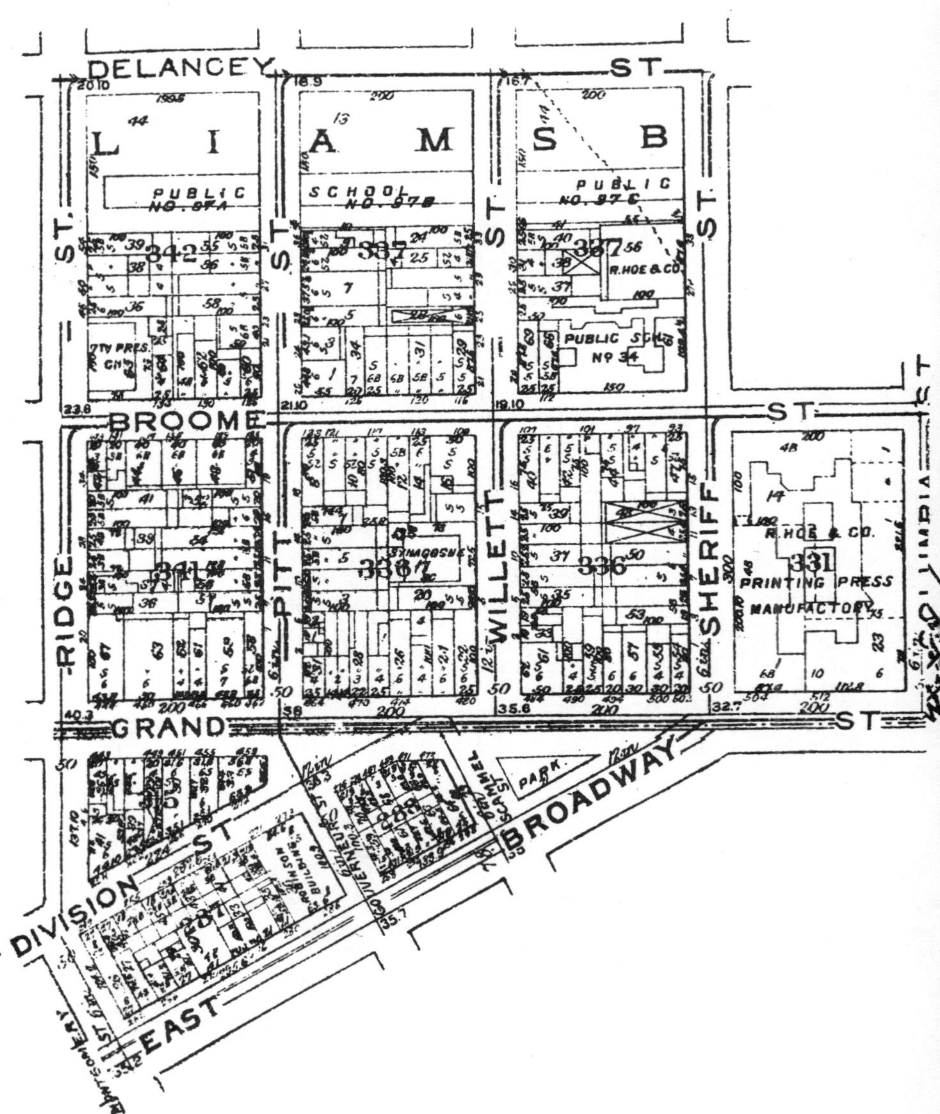
DELANCEY ST.
L I A M S B
PUBLIC SCHOOL NO. 97A
PUBLIC SCHOOL NO. 97B
PUBLIC NO. 97C
R. HOE & CO.
PUBLIC SCHOOL No. 34
342
337
327
7TH PRES. CH.
BROOME ST.
341
337
336
331
SYNAGOGUE
R. HOE & CO.
PRINTING PRESS MANUFACTORY
RIDGE ST.
PITT ST.
WILLETT ST.
SHERIFF ST.
COLUMBIA ST.
GRAND ST.
DIVISION ST.
EAST BROADWAY
PARK
JEFFERSON BUILDING
MONTGOMERY ST.
CLINTON ST.
GOUVERNEUR ST.
SCAMMEL ST.

DELANCY ST
WILLIAMSBURG BRIDGE
BROOME ST
GRAND ST
HESTER ST
BROADWAY
DIVISION ST
EAST
ST
SEWARD PARK
NORFOLK
SUFFOLK
CLINTON
ATTORNEY
RIDGE
CLINTON
POLICE STA #234
HALL
PUBLIC SCH No 92
SYNAGOGUE
PUBLIC SCHOOL No 120
HALL
EMANUEL BAPT. CH.
STATE BANK
ST MARYS R.C. CH.
FIRE DEPT
BANK

The Third Avenue El station at Chatham Square.

Courtesy of the Merlis Collection

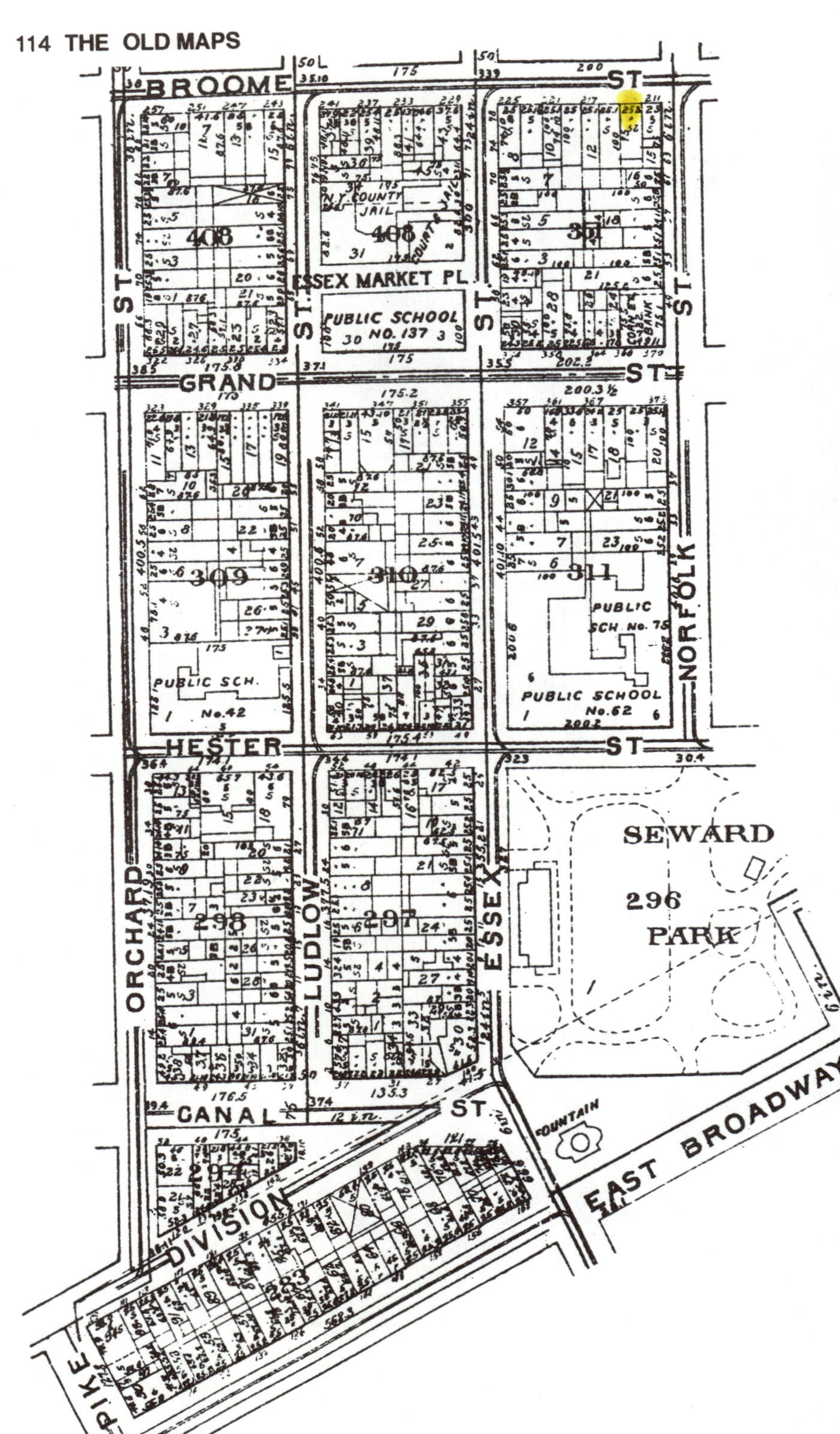
BROOME ST
408
408
ESSEX MARKET PL.
PUBLIC SCHOOL
NO. 137
N.Y. COUNTY JAIL
GRAND ST
ORCHARD ST
LUDLOW ST
ESSEX ST
NORFOLK
309
310
311
PUBLIC SCH. No. 42
PUBLIC SCH. No. 75
PUBLIC SCHOOL No. 62
HESTER ST
298
297
SEWARD
296
PARK
CANAL ST
FOUNTAIN
PIKE
DIVISION
EAST BROADWAY

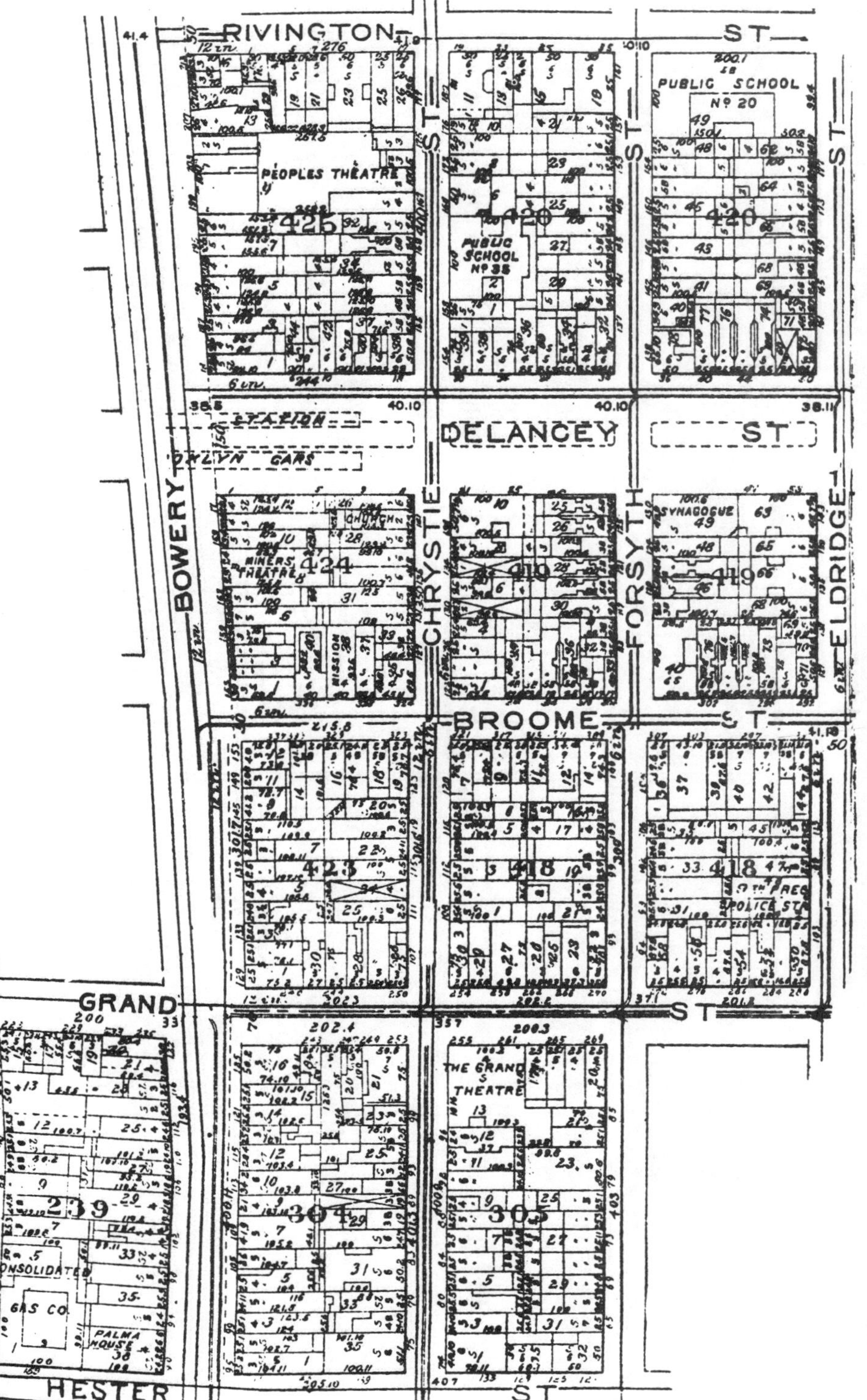
RIVINGTON ST
PUBLIC SCHOOL No 20
PEOPLES THEATRE
425
420
420
BOWERY
CHRYSTIE ST
FORSYTH
ELDRIDGE
PUBLIC SCHOOL No 35
STATION
DELANCEY ST
TROLLEY CARS
CHURCH
MINERS THEATRE
424
410
SYNAGOGUE
419
MISSION
BROOME ST
423
418
418
9TH PREC POLICE STA
GRAND ST
239
304
303
CONSOLIDATED GAS CO.
THE GRAND THEATRE
PALMA HOUSE
HESTER ST

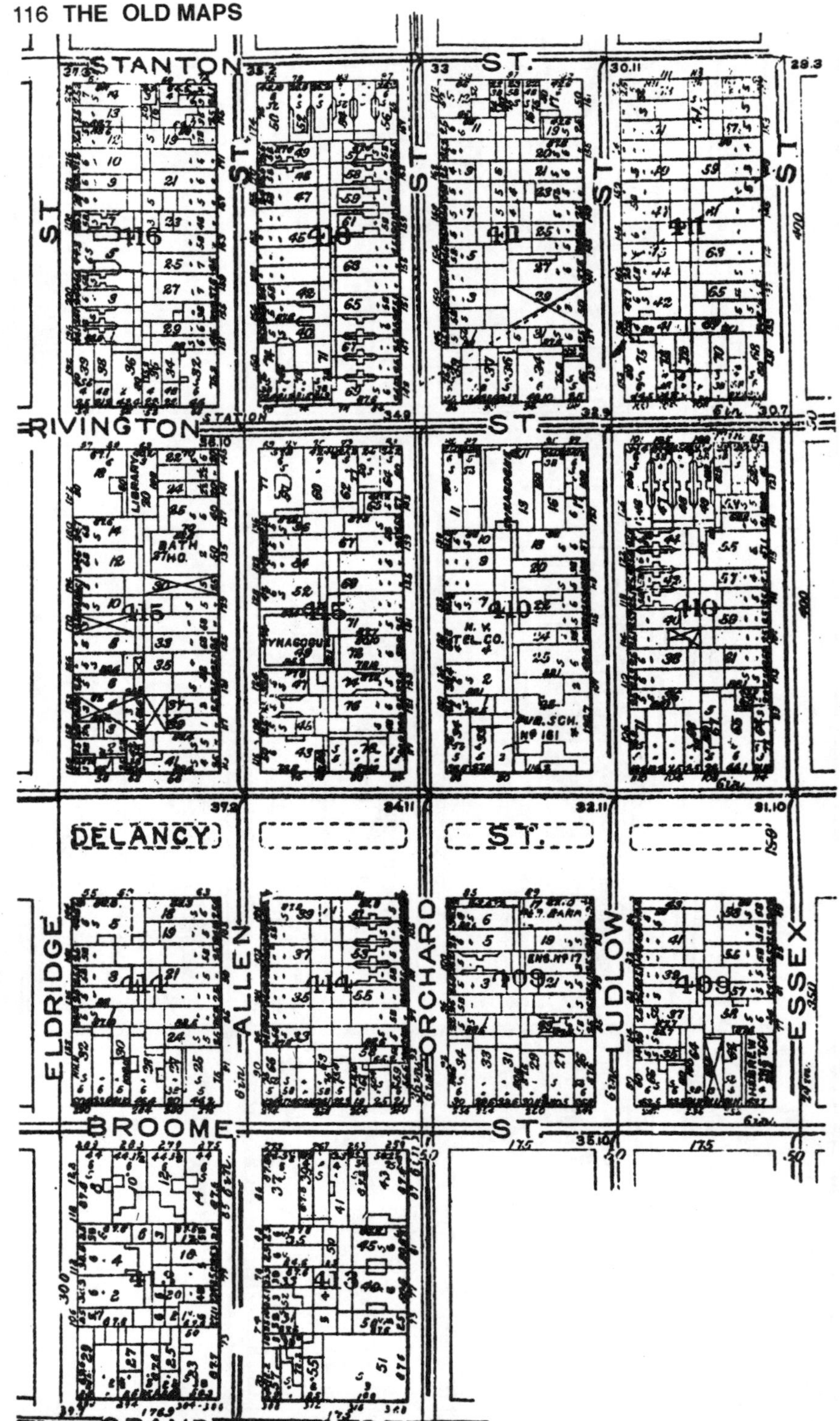
STANTON ST.
RIVINGTON ST.
DELANCY ST.
BROOME ST.
GRAND ST.
ELDRIDGE ST
ALLEN ST
ORCHARD ST
LUDLOW ST
ESSEX ST
LIBRARY
BATH STHO.
SYNAGOGUE
N.Y. TEL. CO.
PUB. SCH. N9 161
ENG. N9 17
HEBREW
116
419
411
411
415
416
410
410
414
414
409
409
413

Hester & Essex Streets in the 1950s.

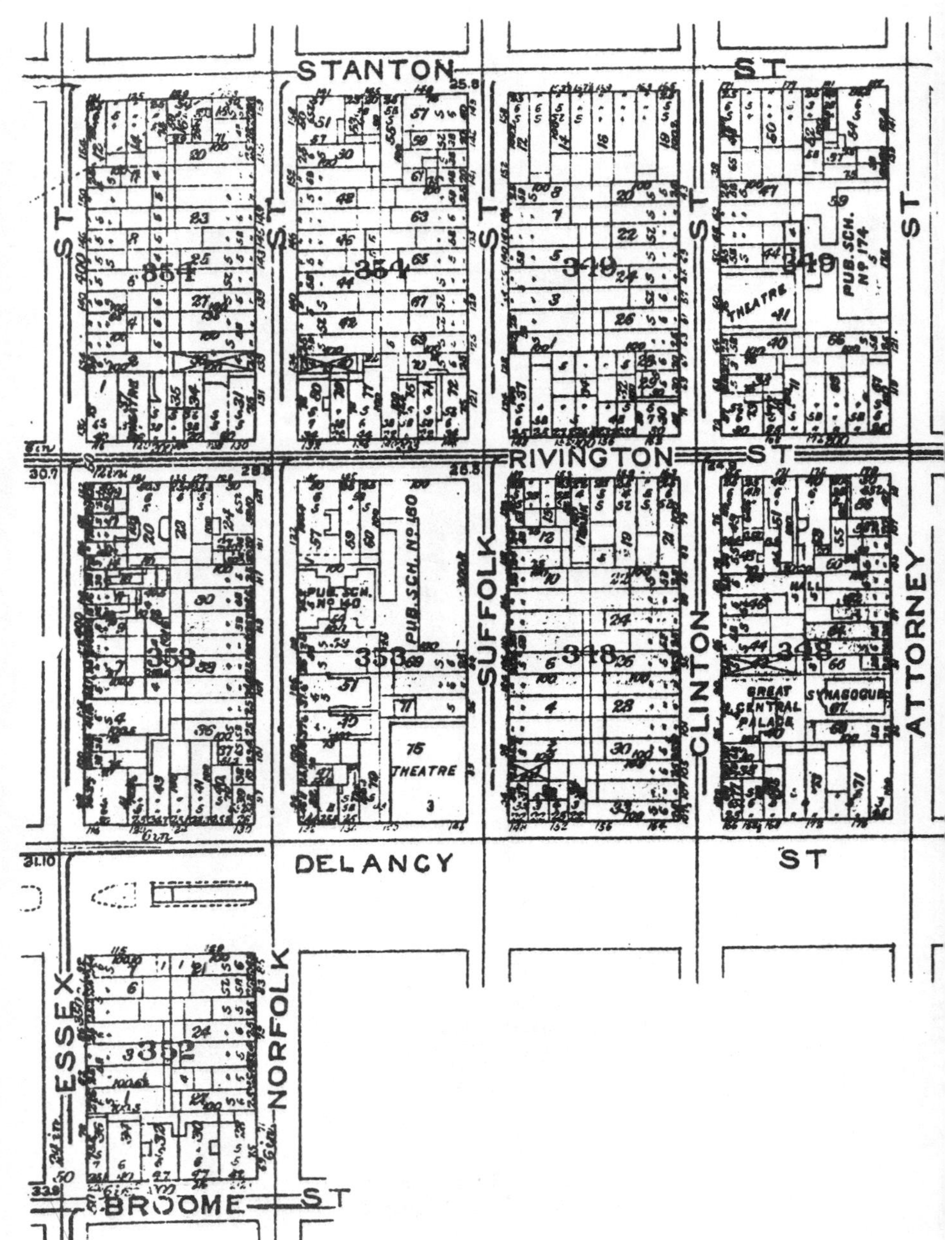

STANTON ST
854
354
349
349
PUB. SCH. N° 174
THEATRE
RIVINGTON ST
ESSEX ST
NORFOLK ST
SUFFOLK
CLINTON ST
ATTORNEY
PUB. SCH. N° 160
353
THEATRE
348
348
GREAT CENTRAL PALACE
SYNAGOGUE
DELANCY ST
352
BROOME ST

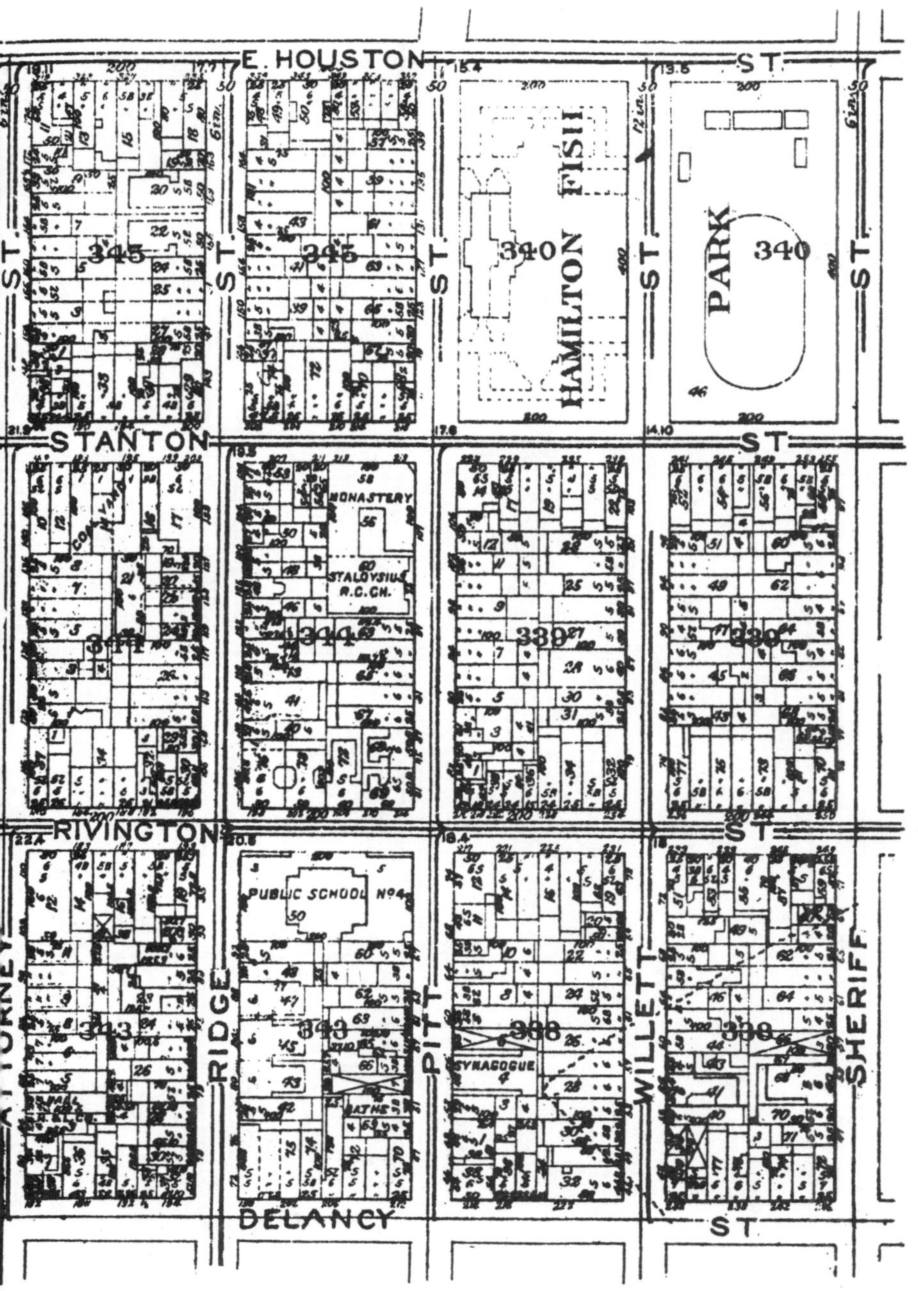
E. HOUSTON
ST.
HAMILTON FISH
340
ST.
PARK
340
ST.
345
345
ST.
STANTON
ST.
CONVENT
MONASTERY
ST ALOYSIUS
R.C. CH.
344
339
330
RIVINGTON
ST.
ATTORNEY
PUBLIC SCHOOL No. 4
50
RIDGE
343
PITT
338
SYNAGOGUE
WILLETT
330
SHERIFF
BATHS
DELANCY
ST.

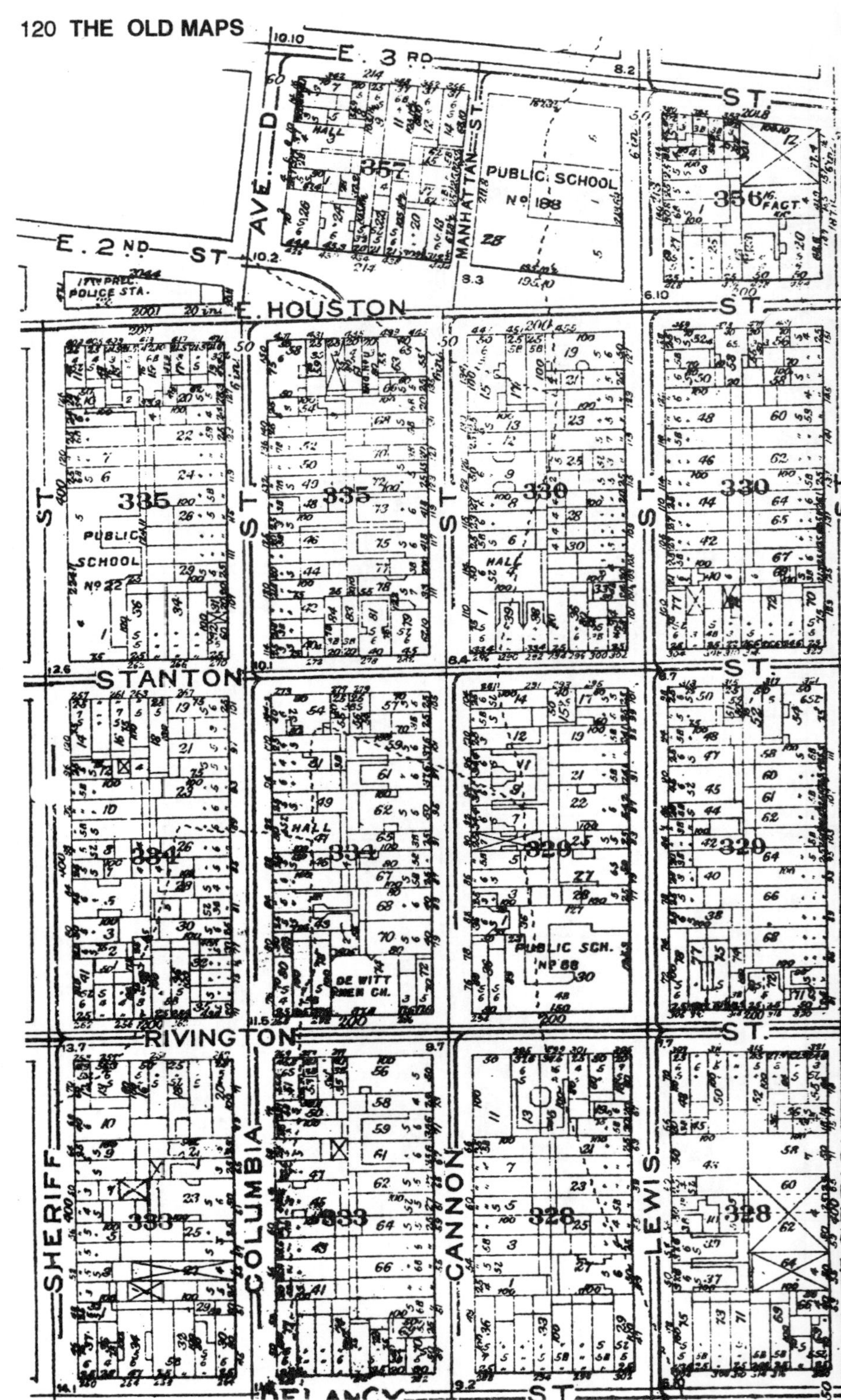
E. 3 RD ST
AVE. D
MANHATTAN ST.
357
PUBLIC SCHOOL No 188
356 FACT.
E. 2ND ST.
17TH PREC. POLICE STA.
E. HOUSTON
335
335
330
330
PUBLIC SCHOOL No 22
ST
HALL
STANTON
334
334
320
329
DE WITT REFM CH.
PUBLIC SCH. No 68
HALL
RIVINGTON ST.
SHERIFF
COLUMBIA
CANNON
LEWIS
333
333
328
328
DELANCEY ST.

The annual Estrog Market assembles at Canal & Essex Streets
on the Sunday(s) following Rosh Hashanah.

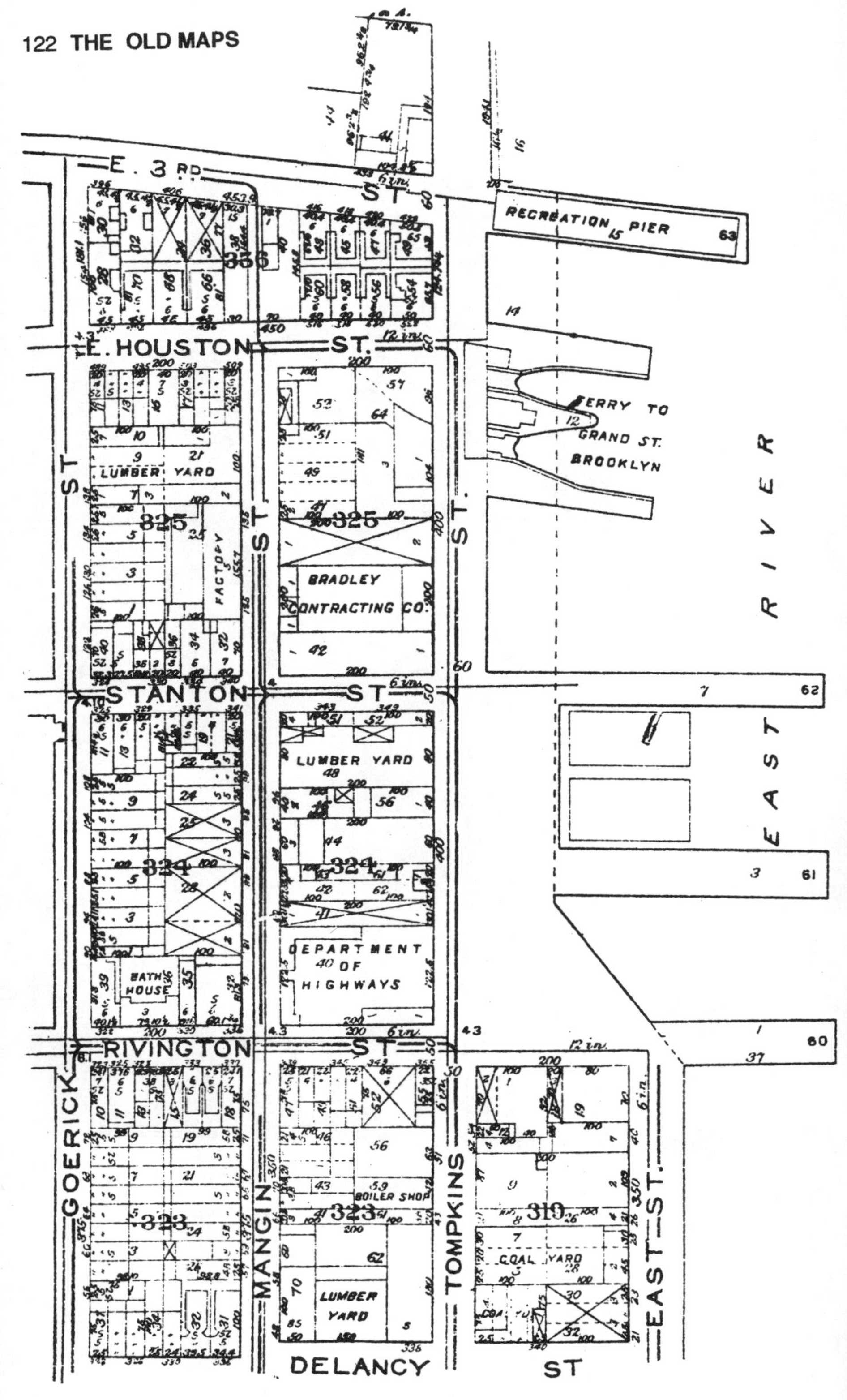
E. 3 RD ST.
RECREATION PIER
63
E. HOUSTON ST.
LUMBER YARD
825
FACTORY
325
BRADLEY
CONTRACTING CO.
FERRY TO
GRAND ST.
BROOKLYN
EAST RIVER
STANTON ST.
62
LUMBER YARD
324
DEPARTMENT
OF
HIGHWAYS
BATH
HOUSE
61
RIVINGTON ST.
60
GOERICK ST.
323
MANGIN ST.
BOILER SHOP
323
LUMBER YARD
TOMPKINS ST.
310
COAL YARD
EAST ST.
DELANCY ST.

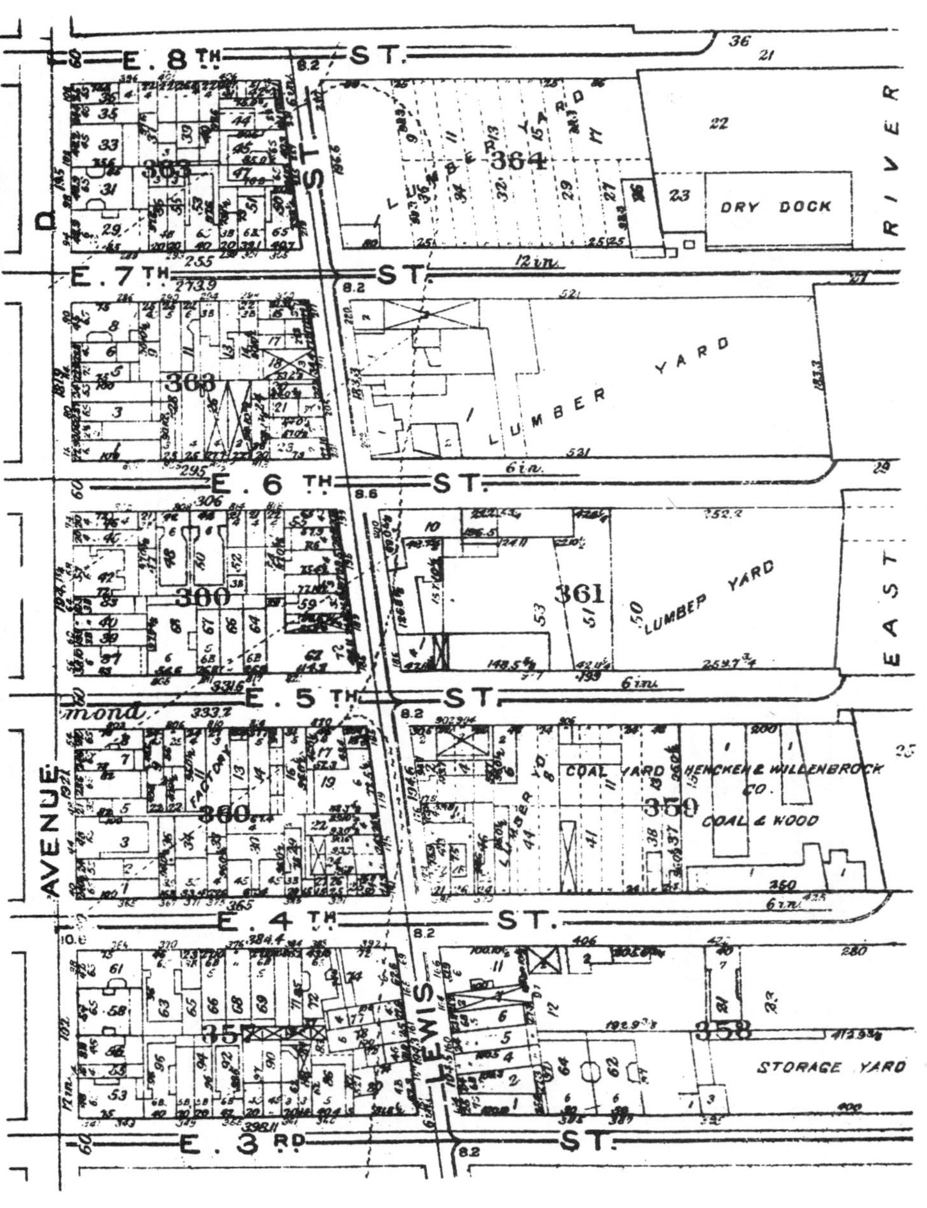
RIVER
DRY DOCK
E. 8TH ST.
364
E. 7TH ST.
LUMBER YARD
363
E. 6TH ST.
361
LUMBER YARD
360
EAST
E. 5TH ST.
mond
FACTORY
362
COAL YARD
HENCKEN & WILLENBROCK CO.
COAL & WOOD
359
LUMBER YD.
E. 4TH ST.
358
STORAGE YARD
357
LEWIS
AVENUE
D
E. 3RD ST.

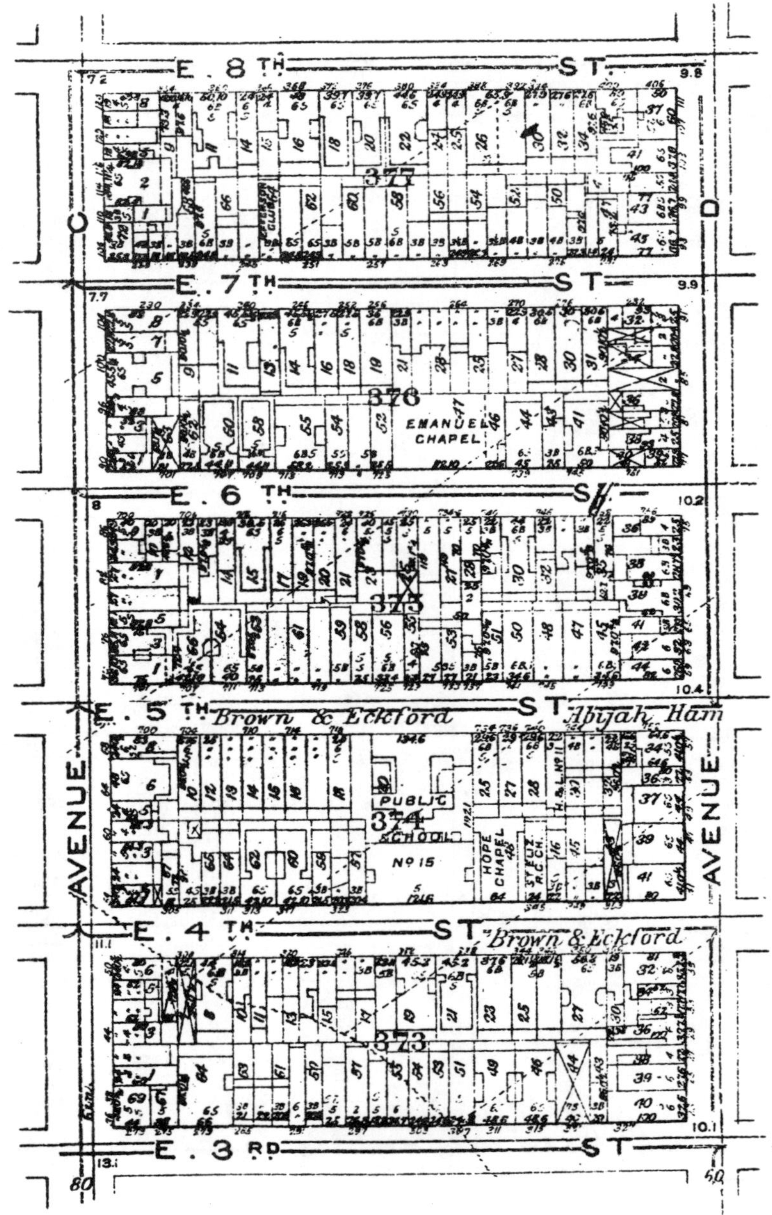
E. 8TH ST.
E. 7TH ST.
E. 6TH ST.
E. 5TH ST.
E. 4TH ST.
E. 3RD ST.
AVENUE C
AVENUE D
EMANUEL CHAPEL
PUBLIC SCHOOL No 15
HOPE CHAPEL
Brown & Eckford
Abijah Ham
377
376
375
374
373

Allen & Rivington Streets (looking east) in the 1950s

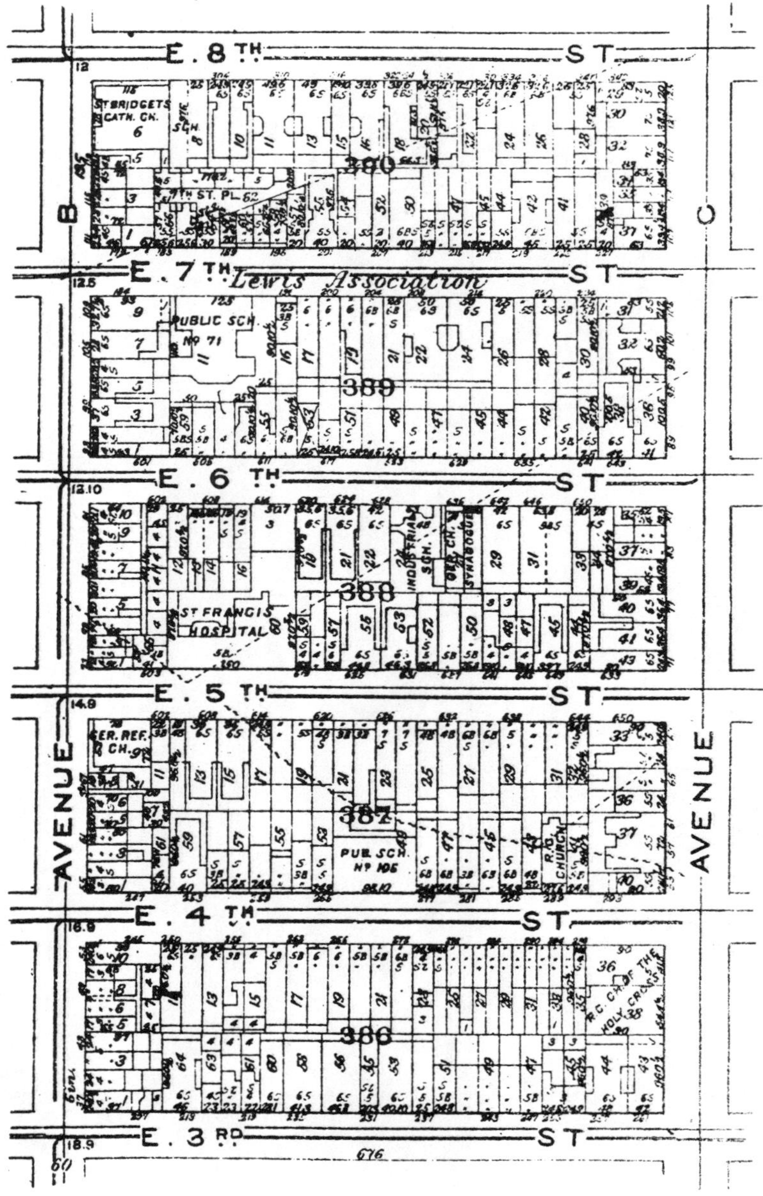

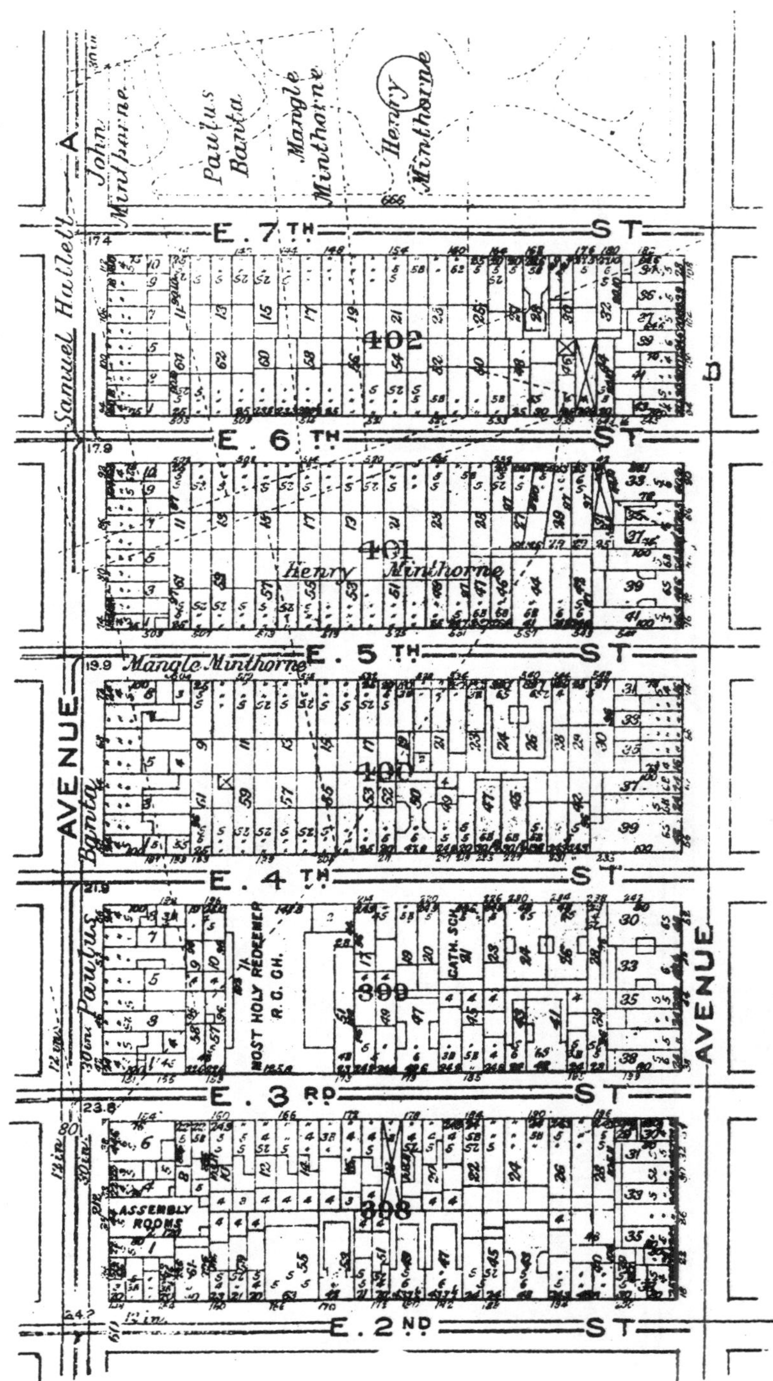
Samuel Hallett
A
John Mindhaarne
Paulus Banta
Mangle Minthorne
Henry Minthorne
E. 7TH ST
402
E. 6TH ST
Henry Minthorne
401
b
Mangle Minthorne
E. 5TH ST
Banta
400
E. 4TH ST
Paulus
MOST HOLY REDEEMER R. C. CH.
CATH. SCH.
399
AVENUE
E. 3RD ST
AVENUE
ASSEMBLY ROOMS
398
E. 2ND ST

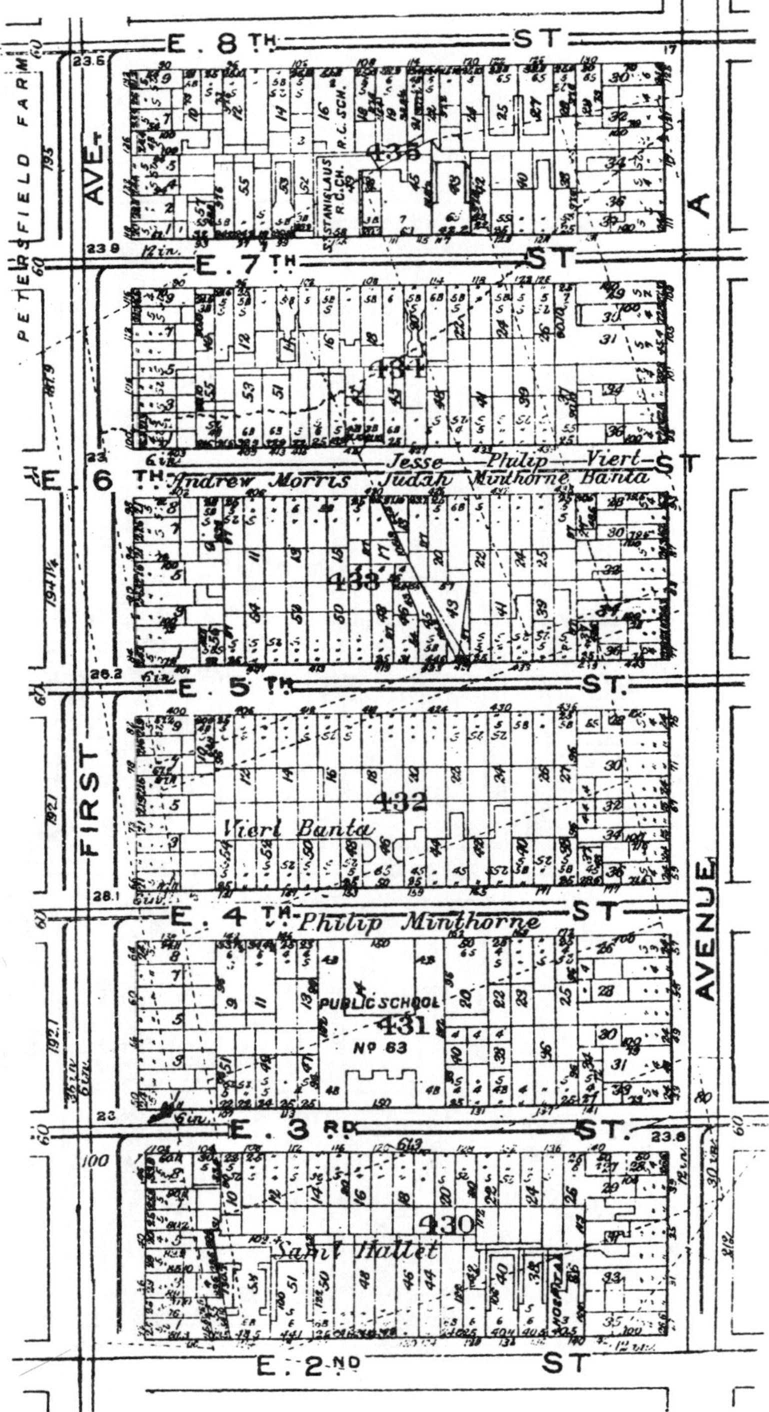
E. 8TH ST
PETERSFIELD FARM
AVE.
A
E. 7TH ST
ST. STANISLAUS R.C.CH.
435
E. 6TH ST
Andrew Morris
Jesse Judah
Philip Minthorne
Viert Banta
433
FIRST
E. 5TH ST
Viert Banta
432
AVENUE
E. 4TH ST
Philip Minthorne
PUBLIC SCHOOL
431
No 63
E. 3RD ST
430
Saml Hallet
E. 2ND ST

Selection of a Lulav prior to the holiday of Succos.

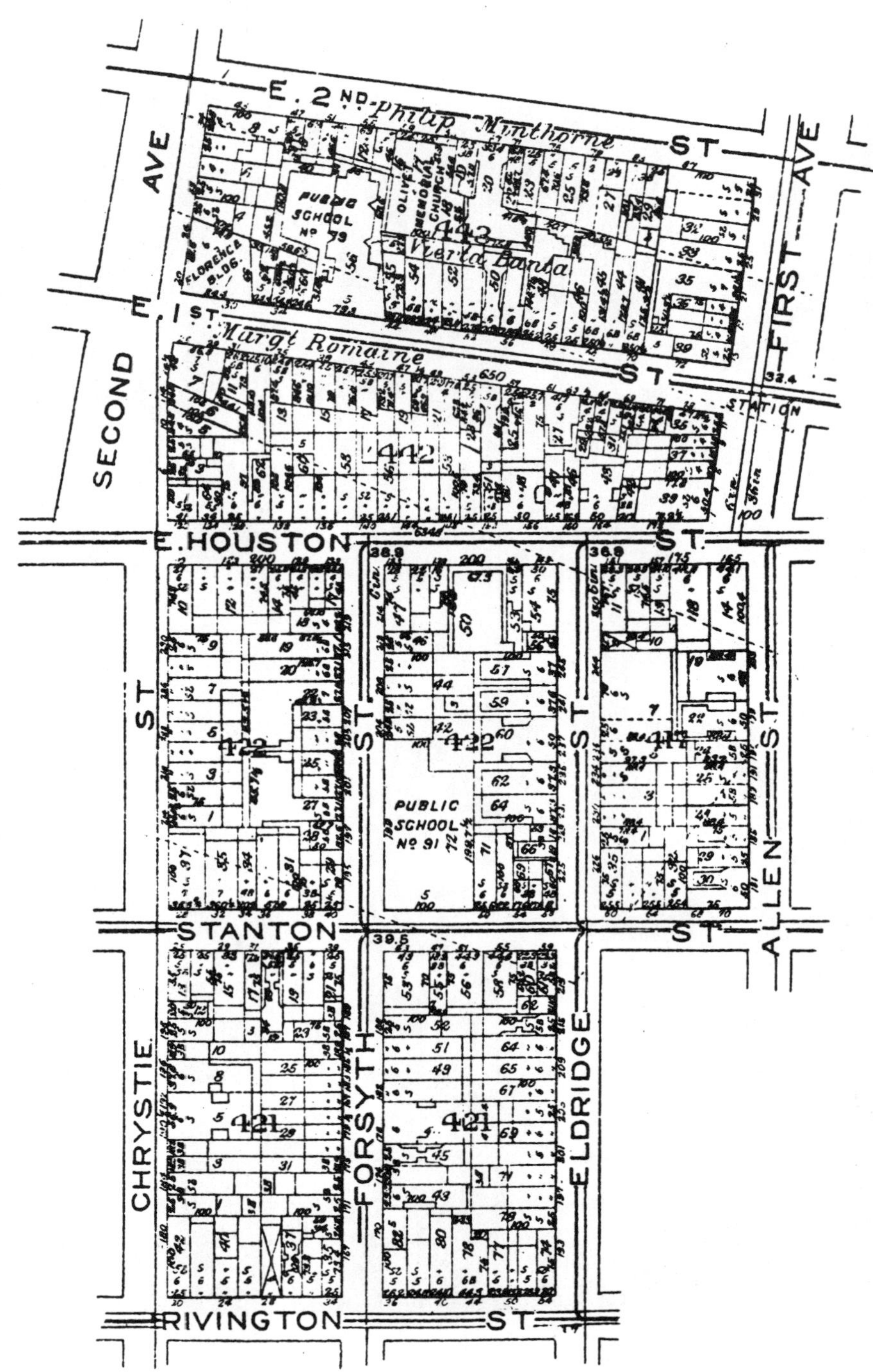
E. 2ND St
Philip Minthorne
AVE
FIRST AVE
PUBLIC SCHOOL NO 79
OLIVE MEMORIAL CHURCH
443
Vetta Banta
FLORENCE BLDG
E. 1ST St
Second St
Margt Romaine St
442
STATION
E. HOUSTON St
422
PUBLIC SCHOOL NO 91
412
417
ST
ST
ALLEN ST
STANTON St
CHRYSTIE
FORSYTH
ELDRIDGE
421
421
RIVINGTON ST

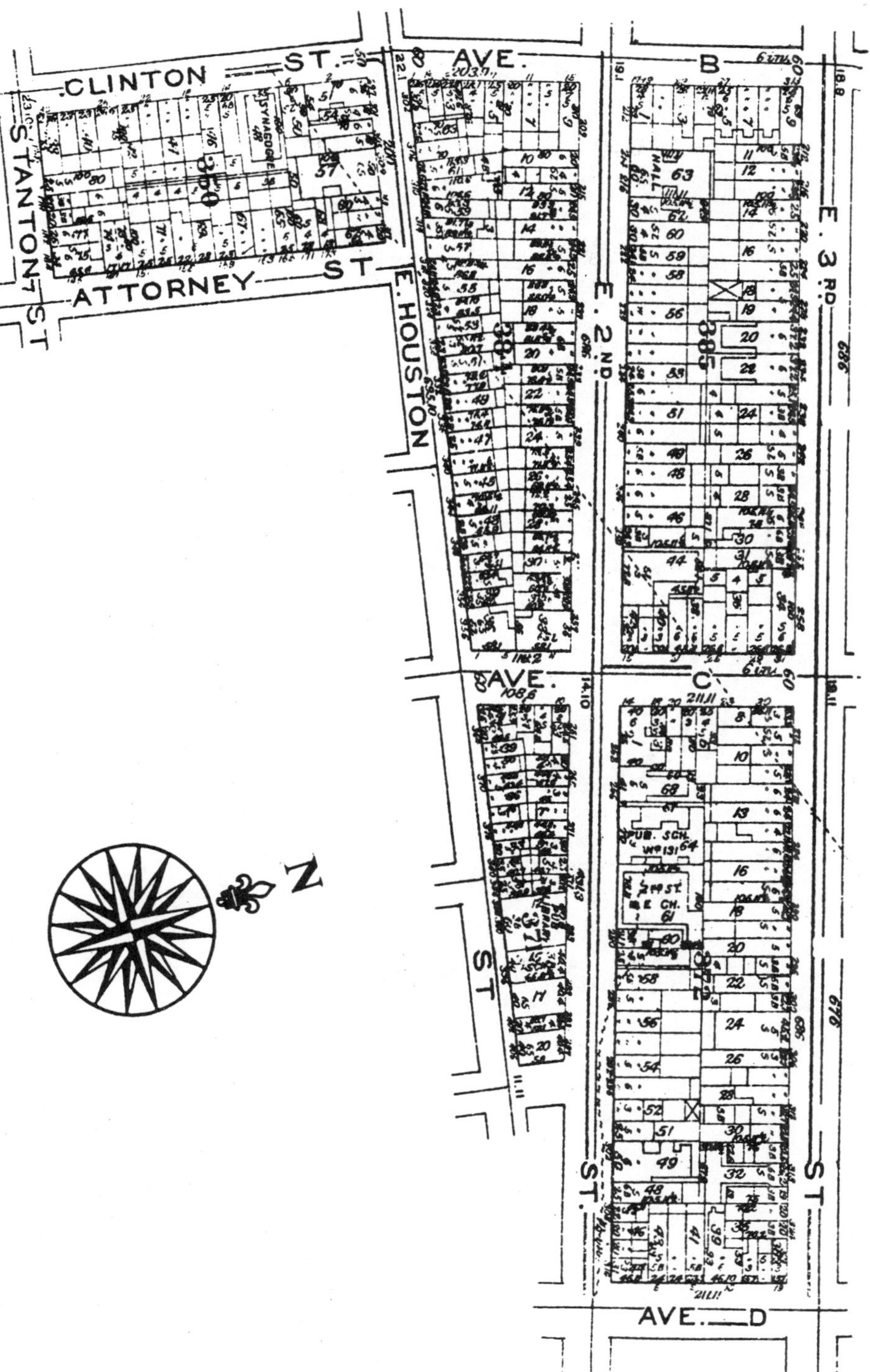
CLINTON ST.
AVE. B
E. 3 RD
STANTON ST.
SYNAGOGUE
ATTORNEY ST.
E. HOUSTON
E. 2 ND
HALL
PUB. SCH. W 131
2ND ST. M.E. CH.
AVE. C
ST.
AVE. D
N

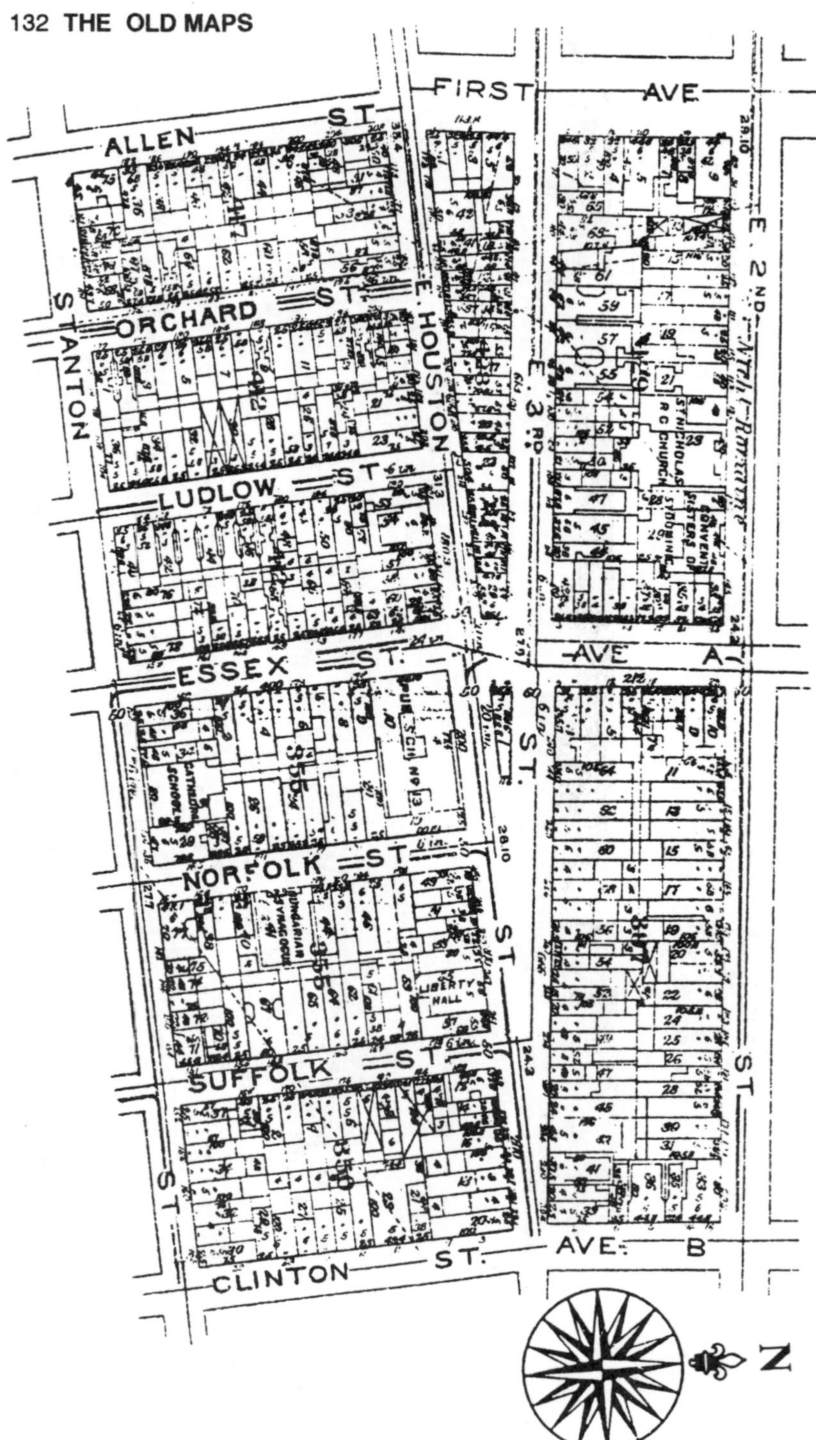
ALLEN ST
ORCHARD ST
LUDLOW ST
ESSEX ST
NORFOLK ST
SUFFOLK ST
CLINTON ST
FIRST AVE
E. HOUSTON ST
E. 3 RD ST
AVE A
AVE B
E. 2 ND
STANTON
ST. NICHOLAS R.C. CHURCH
CONVENT SISTERS OF
LIBERTY HALL
HUNGARIAN SYNAGOGUE
CATHOLIC SCHOOL
PUB. SCH. NO 13
N

Second Avenue El station at Grand Street, circa 1890.

Courtesy of the Museum of the City of New York

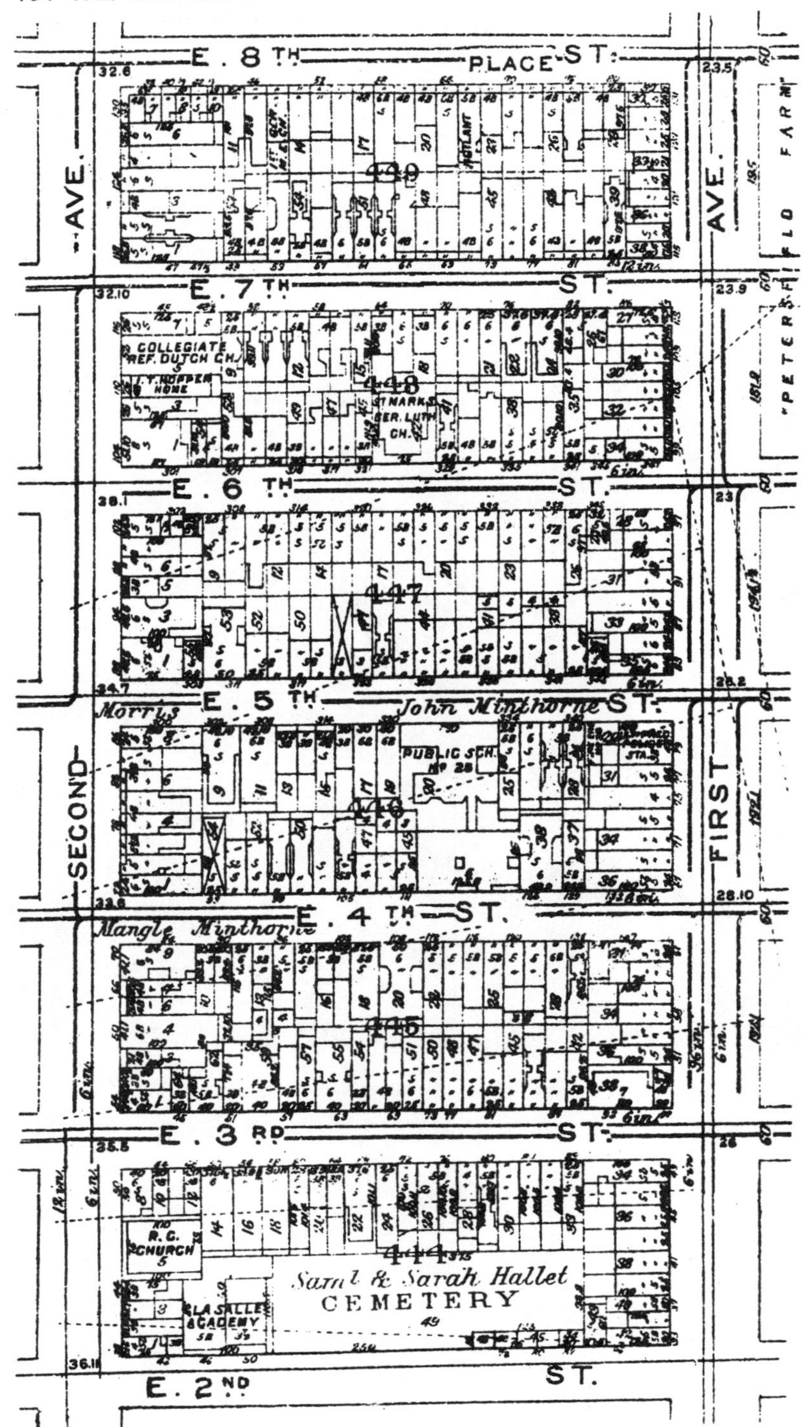
E. 8TH PLACE ST.
AVE.
AVE.
"PETERSFIELD FARM"
E. 7TH ST.
COLLEGIATE REF. DUTCH CH.
I.T. HOPPER HOME
ST. MARKS GER. LUTH. CH.
E. 6TH ST.
Morris
SECOND
E. 5TH John Minthorne ST.
PUBLIC SCH. N? 28
FIRST
E. 4TH ST.
Mangle Minthorne
E. 3RD ST.
R.C. CHURCH
LA SALLE ACADEMY
Sam'l & Sarah Hallet CEMETERY
E. 2ND ST.

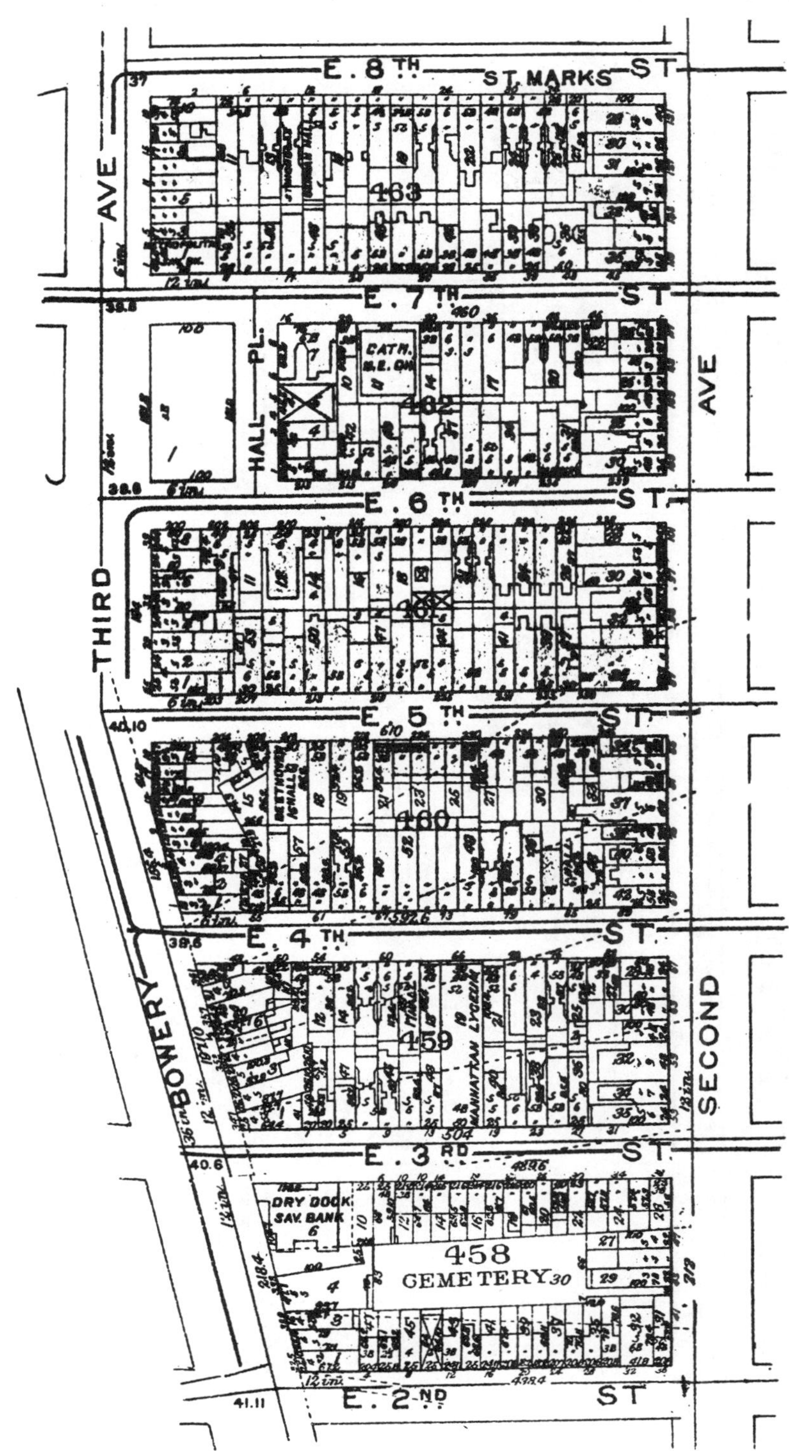
E. 8TH ST MARKS ST
E. 7TH ST
E. 6TH ST
E. 5TH ST
E. 4TH ST
E. 3RD ST
E. 2ND ST
AVE
THIRD
AVE
SECOND
BOWERY
HALL PL.
463
462
461
460
459
458
CEMETERY
DRY DOCK SAV. BANK
CATH. R.E. CH.
BEETHOVEN MÄNNERHALL
MANHATTAN LYCEUM

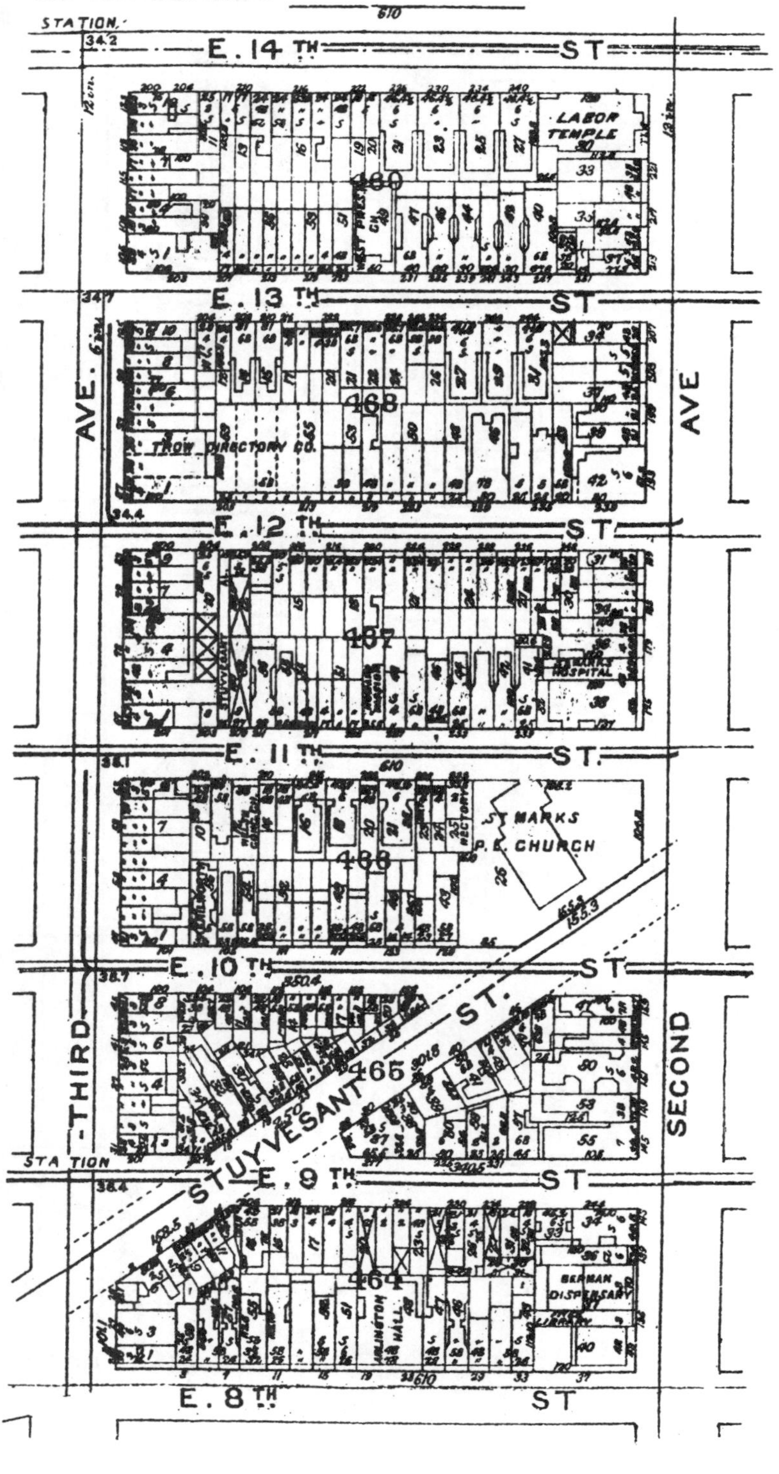

STATION
E. 14 TH ST
LABOR TEMPLE
WEST PRES. CH.
E. 13 TH ST
AVE.
AVE
TROW DIRECTORY CO.
E. 12 TH ST
HOSPITAL
E. 11 TH ST
ST. MARKS P. E. CHURCH
RECTORY
E. 10 TH ST
THIRD
SECOND
STUYVESANT ST.
STATION
E. 9 TH ST
ARLINGTON HALL
GERMAN DISPENSARY
E. 8 TH ST

Typical Street Scene, circa 1925.

Courtesy of the Museum of the City of New York

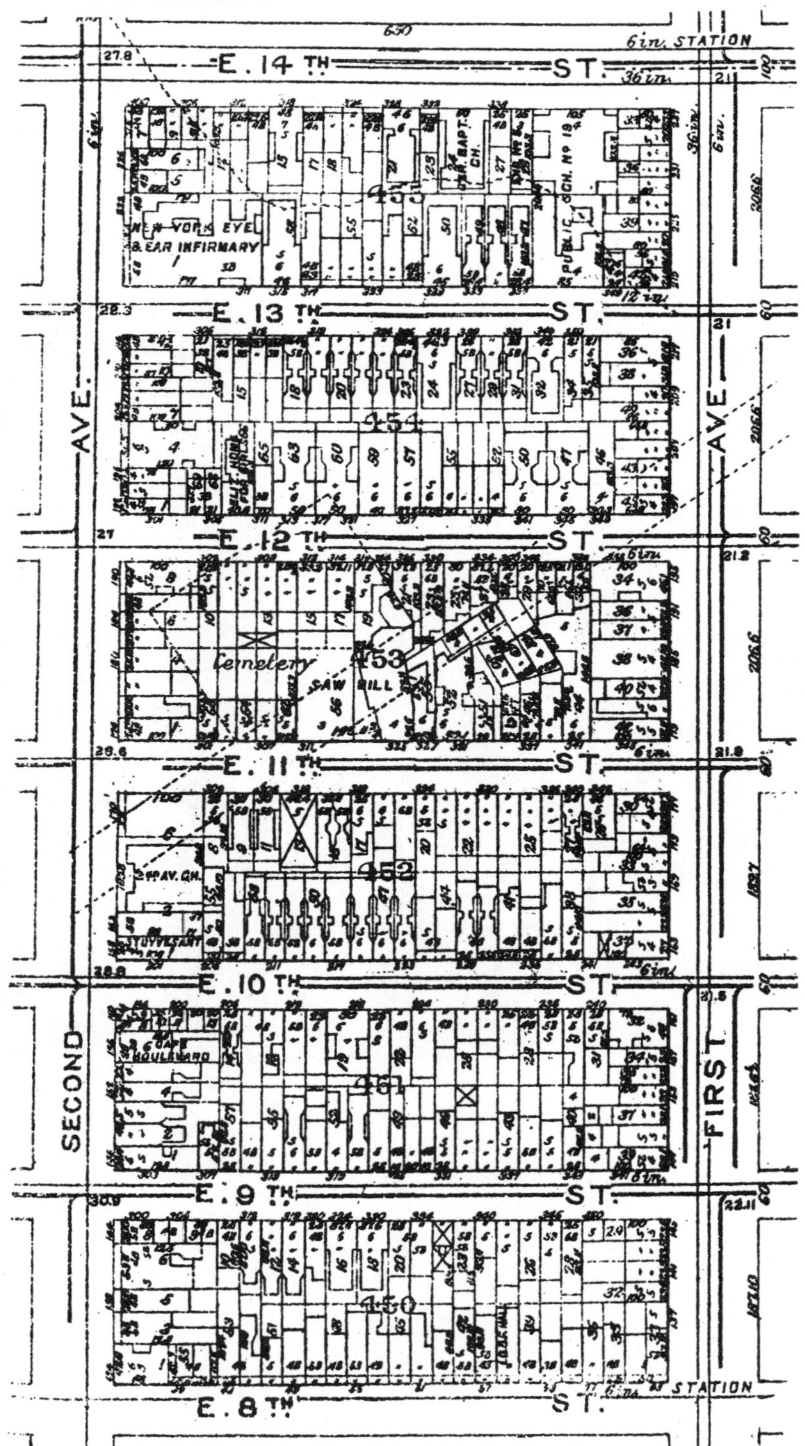
6in. STATION
27.8
E. 14 TH ST.
36in
211
NEW YORK EYE
& EAR INFIRMARY
PUBLIC SCH. No 19
AVE.
28.3
E. 13 TH ST.
451
AVE.
27
E. 12 TH ST.
453
Cemetery
SAW MILL
29.6
E. 11 TH ST.
452
STUYVESANT
SECOND
E. 10 TH ST.
FIRST
45
E. 9 TH ST.
E. 8 TH ST.
STATION

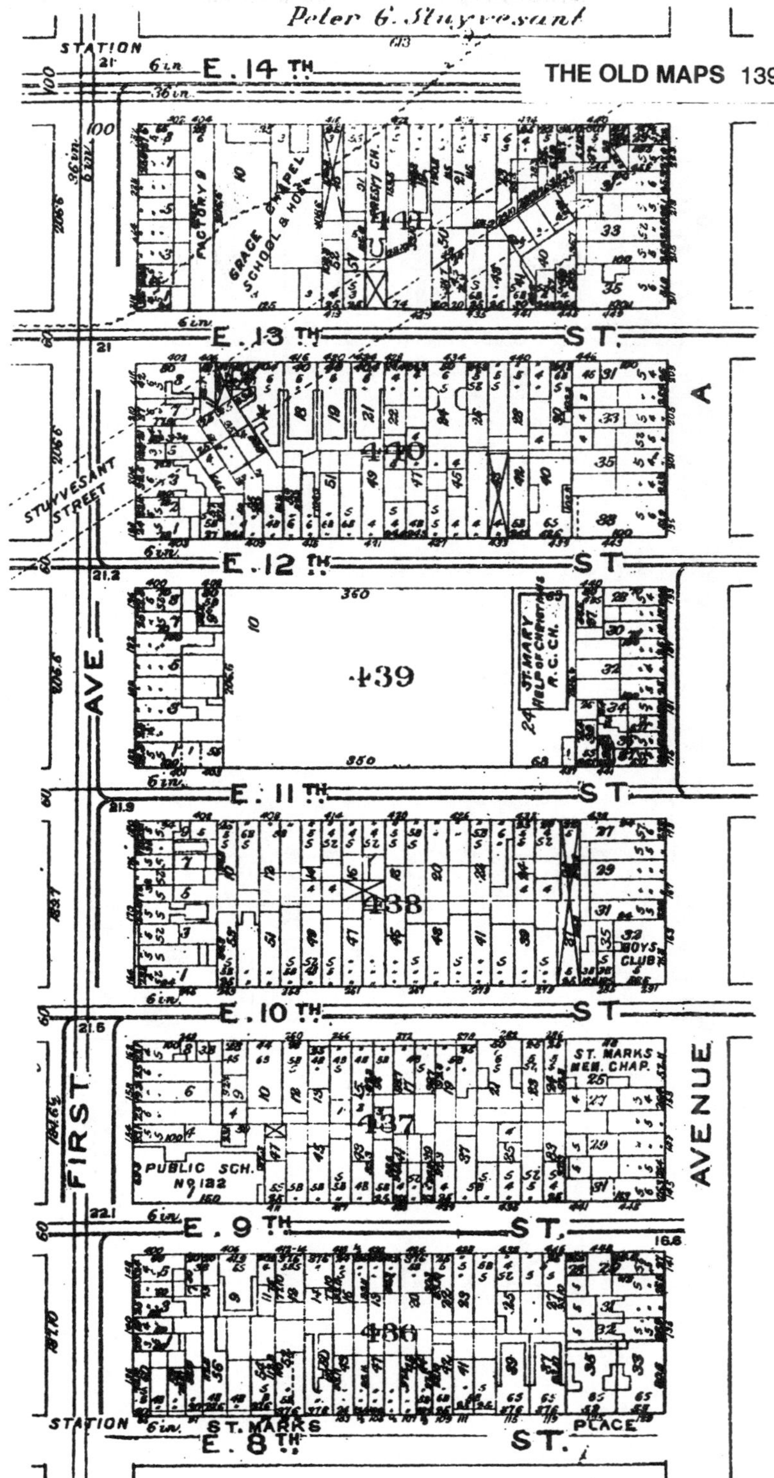
Peter G. Stuyvesant
STATION
E. 14 TH
E. 13 TH ST.
E. 12 TH ST.
E. 11 TH ST.
E. 10 TH ST.
E. 9 TH ST.
E. 8 TH ST.
ST. MARKS PLACE
STATION
FIRST AVE.
A
AVENUE
STUYVESANT STREET
FACTORY
GRACE CHAPEL SCHOOL & HOSP.
441
440
439
438
437
436
ST. MARY HELP OF CHRISTIANS R.C. CH.
ST. MARKS MEM. CHAP.
PUBLIC SCH. NO 122
BOYS CLUB
6 in.
36 in.

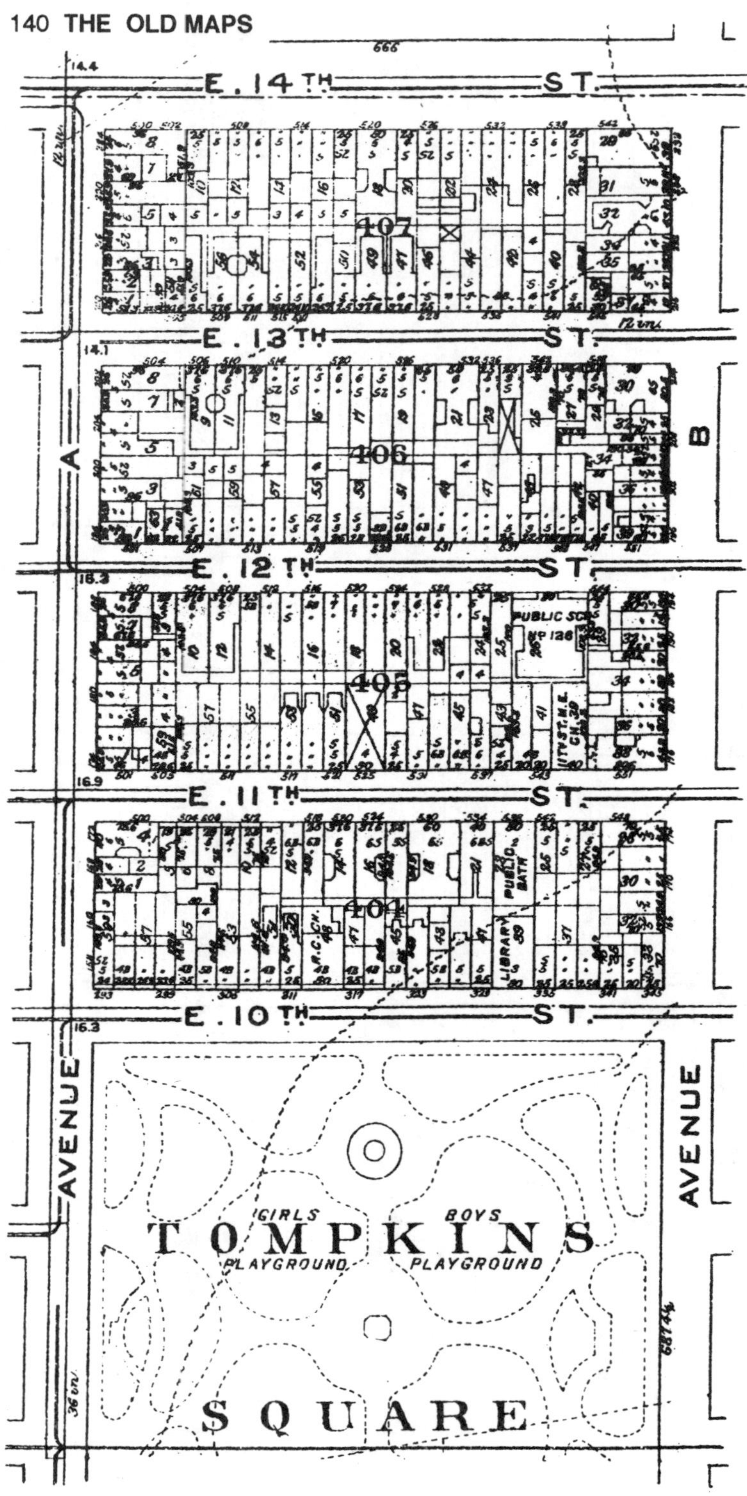
E. 14TH ST.
E. 13TH ST.
E. 12TH ST.
E. 11TH ST.
E. 10TH ST.
AVENUE
A
B
AVENUE
PUBLIC SCH.
N? 126
PUBLIC
BATH
LIBRARY
TOMPKINS
GIRLS
PLAYGROUND
BOYS
PLAYGROUND
SQUARE
407
406
405
404

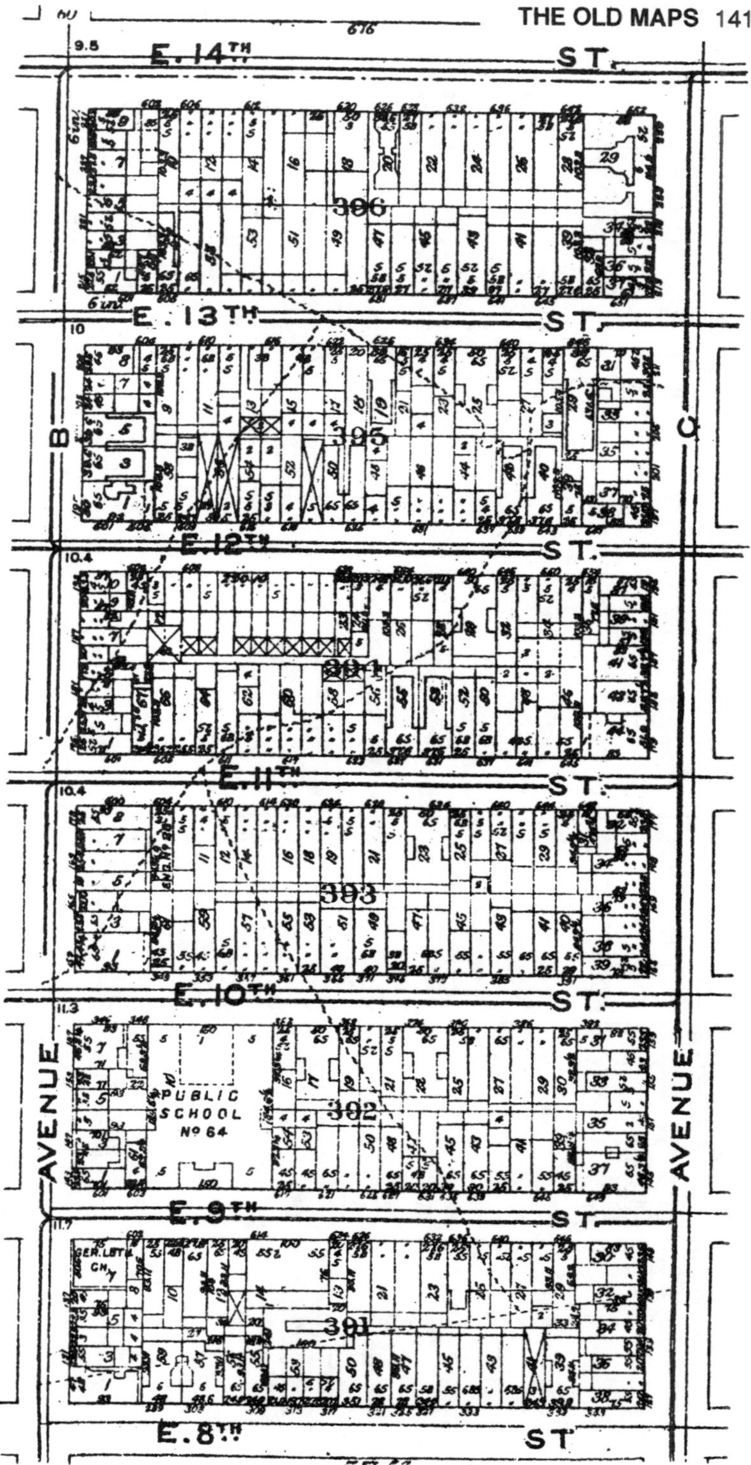

E. 14TH ST.
E. 13TH ST.
E. 12TH ST.
E. 11TH ST.
E. 10TH ST.
E. 9TH ST.
E. 8TH ST.
B AVENUE
C AVENUE
396
395
394
393
392
391
PUBLIC SCHOOL No 64
GER. LUTH. CH.

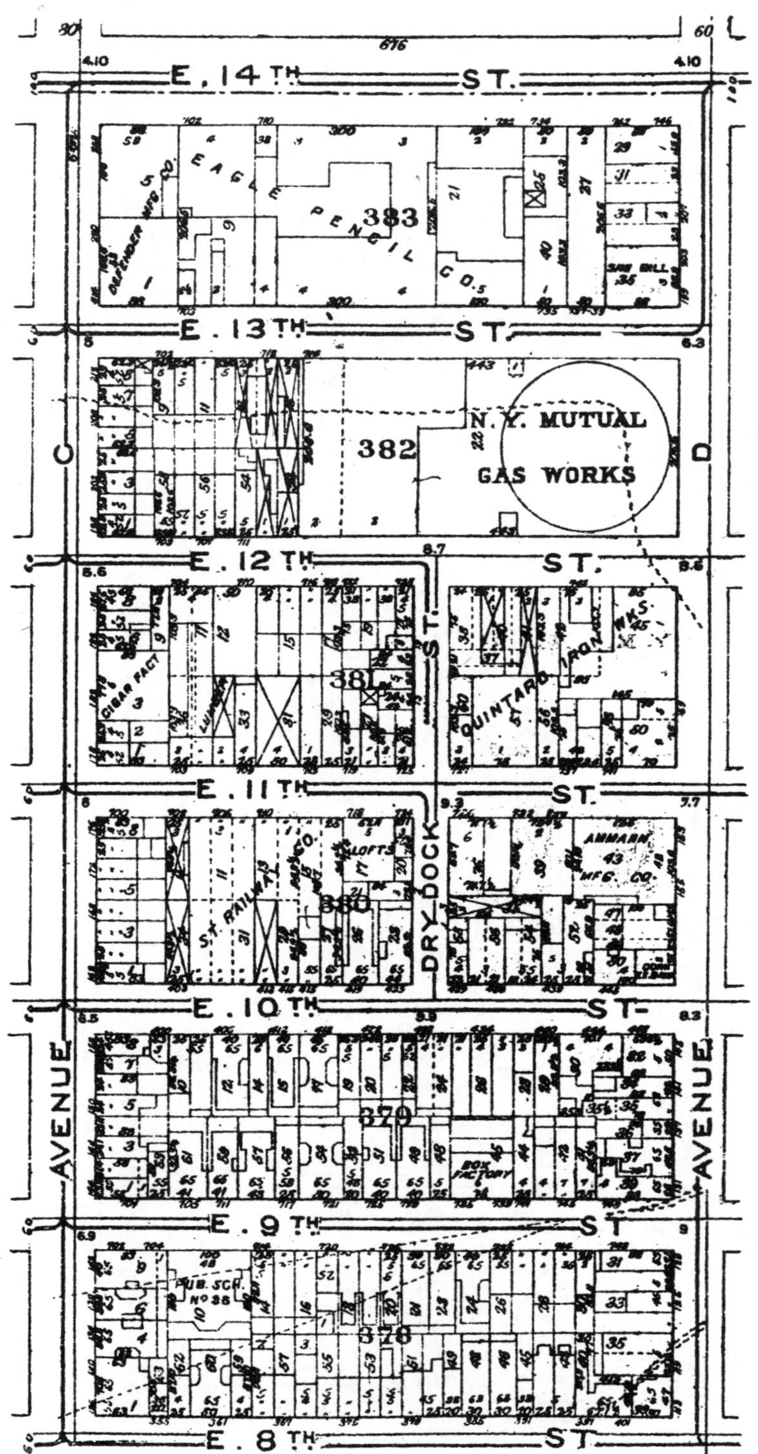
E. 14 TH ST.
EAGLE PENCIL CO.
383
E. 13 TH ST.
C
382
N. Y. MUTUAL GAS WORKS
D
E. 12 TH ST.
CIGAR FACT
381
QUINTARD IRON WKS.
E. 11 TH ST.
ST. RAILWAY DEPOT CO.
LOFTS
380
DRY DOCK
ANMANN MFG. CO.
E. 10 TH ST.
AVENUE
379
BOX FACTORY
AVENUE
E. 9 TH ST.
PUB. SCH. NO 35
378
E. 8 TH ST.

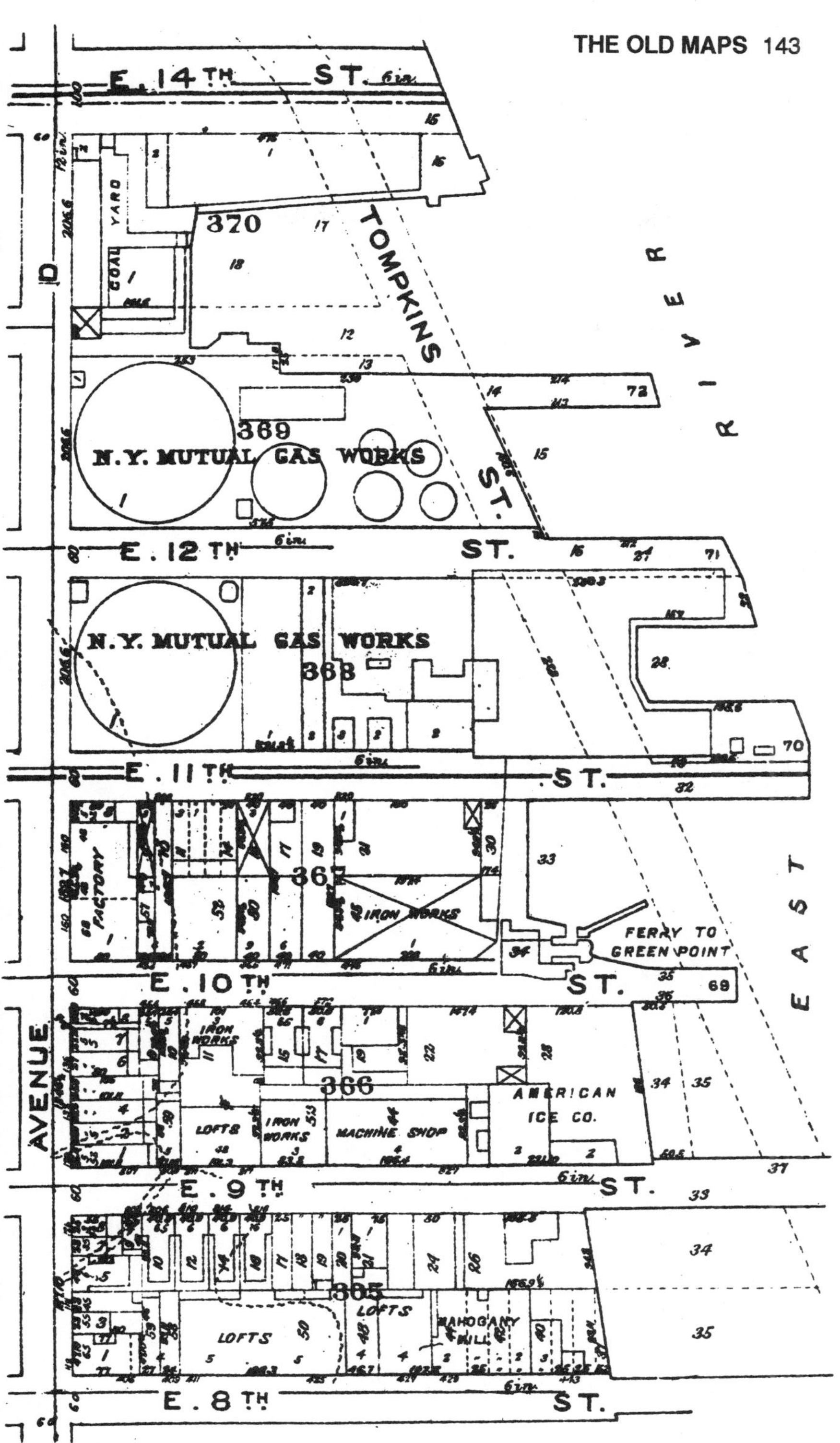
E. 14 TH ST.
TOMPKINS ST.
COAL YARD
370
369
N.Y. MUTUAL GAS WORKS
RIVER
72
E. 12 TH ST.
N.Y. MUTUAL GAS WORKS
368
71
70
E. 11 TH ST.
FACTORY
367
IRON WORKS
FERRY TO GREEN POINT
E. 10 TH ST.
69
IRON WORKS
366
AMERICAN ICE CO.
LOFTS
IRON WORKS
MACHINE SHOP
E. 9 TH ST.
365
LOFTS
LOFTS
MAHOGANY MILL
AVENUE
EAST
E. 8 TH ST.

Biography

Oscar Israelowitz was born in Brussels, Belgium. He has degrees in architecture and geology and has traveled extensively throughout Europe, the United States, Canada, Africa and Israel. He is an architectural consultant by profession and is registered in the Register of Engineers and Architects in Israel.

Some of his architectural projects include the *Synagogue and Holocaust Center* of the Bobover chassidim and the *Yeshiva Rabbi Chaim Berlin*, both in Brooklyn, NY. He has also designed homes and villas for clients in the United States, Haiti and Israel.

Mr. Israelowitz is a professional photographer. His works have been on exhibit at the Whitney Museum of American Art in a show called *Watch the Closing Doors - Mosaics of the New York City Subways* (1973). That exhibit traveled to the Brooklyn Museum and has been incorporated into a permanent exhibition at the New York City Transit Museum. *The Changing Face of New York's Synagogues* was on exhibit at the Yeshiva University Museum in 1976. *Brooklyn: The City of Churches and Synagogues* was on display at Saint Joseph's College Gallery in Brooklyn in 1979 and traveled to the Long Island (now Brooklyn) Historical Society and to the Main Branch of the Brooklyn Public Library at Grand Army Plaza. In all of these exhibitions Mr. Israelowitz served as the guest curator and project coordinator.

Oscar Israelowitz has appeared on several television and radio programs including the *Joe Franklin Show*, NBC's *First Estate - Religion in Review*, and the Ruth Jacobs' *Jewish Home Show*.

In more recent years, Mr. Israelowitz has been conducting tours of the Lower East Side, Ellis Island and chassidic neighborhoods in Brooklyn. These tours have been written-up in *New York Magazine*, the *Washington Post*, the *New York Times*, the *Los Angeles Times*, the *Chicago Tribune* and *Crain's New York Business*.

TOURS OF JEWISH NEW YORK

LOWER EAST SIDE
This two-hour walking tour includes stops at the old Jewish Daily Forward Building, Seward Park's *Chazir Mark*, the Educational Alliance with its Hall of Fame and Chaim Gross Gallery, Shteeble Row, the Jewish Mural at the Bialystoker Home for the Aged, the last boys' yeshiva in the neighborhood, the Eldridge Street Synagogue, Orchard Street and, of course, Guss' Pickles with its outdoor pickle barrels.

JEWISH HERITAGE TRAIL
This two-hour walking tour includes stops at the Jewish Plymouth Rock, Fraunces Tavern, site of North America's first synagogue, Federal Hall - where George Washington was inaugurated first President of the United States, the New York Stock Exchange, Bowling Green, the Federal Reserve Bank - where Nazi gold was stored, Castle Clinton, Emma Lazarus' historic plaque, the Jerusalem Grove and the new Museum of Jewish Heritage - A Living Memorial to the Holocaust.
Note: Tour does not include entrance to the Museum of Jewish Heritage.

ELLIS ISLAND
This three-hour tour includes a ferry ride past the Statue of Liberty and a walking tour on Ellis Island with its Museum of Immigration and Wall of Honor, with over 400,000 names. The tour includes a visit to the archaeological remains of Fort Gibson, an exciting film about how the 12 million immigrants arrived and were processed, and a stop in the Great Hall with its magnificent Guastavino vaulted ceiling and beautiful chandeliers.

CHASSIDIC NEIGHBORHOODS OF BROOKLYN

This four-hour bus and walking tour includes visits to the Satmar Chassidim in Williamsburg, the Bobover Chassidim in Borough Park and the Lubavitcher Chassidim in Crown Heights. See the great synagogues established by each group. Depending on the time of year when visiting, see the hundreds of *succahs* built on specially-designed terraces, visit a matzoh factory and watch matzohs being created within the prescribed 18 minutes, and visit a mikveh and the Lubavichter Museum.

SYNAGOGUES OF NEW YORK

This four-hour bus tour includes visits to some of the prominant congregations in the city such as the Spanish and Portuguese Synagogue, Temple Emanu-El, the Central Synagogue, B'nai Jeshurun, the Bialystoker Synagogue, the Civic Center Synagogue - which seems to float between two century-old loft buildings, and Congregation Habonim - founded by Holocaust survivors and includes stone fragments of synagogues burned on Kristallnacht.
Note: Some congregations allow visits only on Sundays while others only allow visits on weekdays. Three or four synagogues would be included in each tour.

NOTE: These tours are designed for groups of ten or more.

ISRAELOWITZ TOURS

P.O.Box 228 Brooklyn, NY 11229
Tel. (718) 951-7072

Index